a memoir

JACK WHYTE

FORTY YEARS IN CANADA

JACK WHYTE

a memoir

FORTY YEARS IN CANADA

JACK WHYTE

VANCOUVER • VICTORIA • CALGARY

Heritage House Publishing Company Ltd.

#108 – 17665 66A Avenue	PO Box 468
Surrey, BC V3S 2A7	Custer, WA
www.heritagehouse.ca	98240-0468

Library and Archives Canada Cataloguing in Publication
Whyte, Jack, 1940–
Jack Whyte: forty years in Canada: a memoir. — 1st ed.

ISBN 978-1-894974-22-6

1. Whyte, Jack, 1940–. 2. Scottish Canadians—Biography. 3.Immigrants—Canada—Biography.
4. Authors, Canadian (English)—20th century—Biography. I. Title. II. Title: Forty years in Canada.
PS8595.H947Z465 2007   C813'.54   C2007-905398-X

Library of Congress Control Number: 2006932763

Cover design by Jacqui Thomas
Front cover: Publicity photo from 2005. Back cover (clockwise from left): Looking like his
character Publius Varrus (Halloween 1993); signing his latest book at Book Expo Canada in 2006;
in full regimental garb, in 1973; his first publicity still in 1968.
All photos courtesy of the author unless otherwise noted.

Printed in Canada

This book has been produced on 100% post-consumer recycled paper,
processed chlorine free and printed with vegetable-based dyes.

Heritage House acknowledges the financial support for its publishing program
from the Government of Canada through the Book Publishing Industry Development
Program (BPIDP), Canada Council for the Arts, and the province of British Columbia
through the British Columbia Arts Council and the Book Publishing Tax Credit.

 Canada Council **Conseil des Arts**
for the Arts **du Canada**    BRITISH COLUMBIA
ARTS COUNCIL

To my wife, Beverley,
and to all the friends I have made and known
in Canada over the course of the past four decades.
You may not find your name in this book, but you might
well recognize events and occasions.

TABLE OF CONTENTS

POEMS

INTRODUCTION

I started to put together this compendium early in 2003—it may even have been in 2002—and it remained in flux, changing its parameters and its composition almost incessantly, until the summer of 2006, when it finally settled down and assumed a shape that my publisher and I believed we could live with in relative harmony. Although it has continued to evolve, at least its progress has been more disciplined, confined to the single petri dish we dumped it into once we knew what we would finally be dealing with. So what *are* we dealing with here?

Since word leaked out that I was writing this book, I have been astonished and sometimes dismayed by the number of people who assume that because this work is not fiction, and because it is about me, it must therefore be an autobiography. Not so. This is not an autobiography. An autobiography is, by definition, the story of one's own life up to the time of writing—death seems to have a highly deleterious effect on writers' output—and readers expect the writer to be someone who has achieved enough within his or her lifetime to make others want to read that personal perspective on the events, trivial and otherwise, that shaped them. There is a distressing trend today among young people—so-called celebrities—to generate autobiographies at a young age and with the active cooperation of a ghost writer, both of which elements seem to me to be at odds with the very definition of *auto*biography.

But this book is not an autobiography. It is a memoir, a collection of personal, often trivial reminiscences of events and times that have left indelible impressions upon me since I arrived in Canada from Britain 40 years ago and discovered for the first time what people meant when they talked about "God's country." Before then, not knowing any better, I had thought the term referred to the United States, but in July 1967 I came to realize that I had been wrong for years. And once I realized that, I kept looking around and taking note of what was here. Sometimes my note-taking was specific and meticulous, sometimes much less precise, more concerned with impressions and emotions. Always, however, it was inspired by the simple grandeur of this country, and the often majestic sweep of times, places and events that makes life in Canada something to celebrate and write about, and something to be grateful for. Politicians and public figures come and go—and more than a few have done precisely that since I got here—but amazingly, average Canadians have not changed much in those 40 years, despite the fact that the world in which they live has changed in ways that sometimes appear unbelievable. They may be a bit more diversified nowadays, perhaps more politically correct (although this is an attribute I have grown to loathe, because it simply cannot coexist with any form of humour), certainly more sophisticated and even sensitive in certain areas, but despite all the changes that have come down the pike, every Canadian I know could look at some aspect of this country at least once every day and think, "Wow, look at that!"

And yet many of them don't. It has been my experience that it often takes a newcomer to point out the wonder of what some Canadians have come to take for granted. Once they hear the awe and admiration, the sheer wonder, in a stranger's voice describing something magnificent that they themselves have overlooked for years, they sit up and take notice. But it takes fresh eyes to draw their attention to the richness and profusion of blessings strewn all around this country.

One of the most eye-popping examples of that for me was in 1985, when I worked for several months with a New Westminster man called William E. (Bill) McKinney. He was known to everyone as "the Colonel" because he had actually been the honorary lieutenant-colonel and honorary colonel of the Royal Westminster Regiment of New Westminster for more than 20 years.

I had taken a contract to research and write the corporate history of Johnston Terminals Ltd., a Vancouver-based consortium of transportation companies, in anticipation of its 75th year of operations, and the Colonel, who was then in his 70s and serving on the board of directors, was assigned to act as my liaison with the old guard Johnston employees, introducing me to them officially and in person and making sure I had access to everyone I wanted to interview. I could not have had a better guide: Bill knew everybody still alive who had ever been connected with the company, and his reputation was such that no one was unwilling to meet with us. He had been an executive member of the Johnston board of directors for many years, having started his career with the organization as sales manager on his return from the Second World War in 1946. He looked exactly as I expected an honorary colonel to look: tall, slim, distinguished and dignified, with a silver moustache, an imposing beak of a nose and a no-nonsense air of utter competence. He had never been the type to suffer fools gladly, and for the first few weeks he was visibly patient but quiet most of the time, keeping his expression neutral and noncommittal and holding his opinion of what I was doing closely to his chest.

It irked him, of course, that I knew nothing about the business of Johnston Terminals, for he regarded its people and employees as his own family, just as he regarded and felt responsible for the personnel of his beloved Westminster Regiment. He was outraged that the new management had brought in—from out of province yet—a fancy-dan, supposedly professional writer to handle a story that he believed could and should have been written by one of his own people. And initially he considered my questions and interview techniques a complete waste of time, because my questions were so painstaking, mundane and elementary, all of them predicated on my need for the interviewees to understand my ignorance and take care to explain things carefully to me.

And then one bright summer morning, sitting outside on the patio of one of his favourite restaurants, where he could smoke his pipe, he looked at me through a cloud of smoke and said, "Y' know, I wasn't in favour of this at all, but I'll be damned if I'm not learning more than I ever knew about this company, just from sitting listening to you doing these damned interviews."

He had earned—and learned—a job as sales manager back in the 1940s, and he had been growing with it ever since, seeing everything connected to the company as it related to his daily interests—sales and marketing. Now, through my dogged questions and the remembered experiences of other veteran Johnston employees, he was seeing everything in an entirely new and different light.

The ice was broken that morning, and in the months that followed I derived immense pleasure from seeing the Colonel's increasing delight at discovering that the story of Johnston Terminals was actually the story of British Columbia; that it was Johnston's people, to a major extent, who literally pioneered the expansion and conversion of the old cord-road logging routes of the west coast into today's highway system and, by transporting, warehousing and distributing goods and material, brought prosperity to the province in the first half of the 20th century. He had always felt pride and a sense of achievement in his job and his success, but he had never really *looked*, in all those years, at what was actually there, or at what he and his colleagues had derived from and achieved for British Columbia and, by extension, for Canada.

This was not the first instance of that kind. By the time I met Bill McKinney, I had long since come to accept that I had a knack for pointing out things to Canadians that they might have seen countless times before but never really noticed. It had become a passion of mine to elbow the collective Canadian psyche, to say, "Hey, look over there; isn't that amazing?" I still love doing that, because people look where I point and they say, "Wow!", and the awe in their voices is always mixed with wide-eyed amazement and a hint of dawning pride that this thing, this phenomenon, whatever it might have been at a particular time, is *theirs*.

My compulsion to do this, to seek those "wows," was the genesis of this book, because after three and a half decades of composing verse and taking notes, I had accumulated a collection of *stuff*—mainly narrative poetry, written for fun because I love the form, style and tradition of it. In fact, somewhere amid the wows and the elbowing, I launched a one-man crusade to rescue narrative verse from postmodernist oblivion. Whenever I was invited to recite, I readily accepted. One day, at a writers' festival in Salmon Arm on the Shuswap Lake in BC, a gentleman came up to me and said he had enjoyed listening to my recitation of narrative poems at an event the previous evening. He asked if I had ever attempted to have them published. I laughed at the thought and asked him if he had any idea how small the market is for poetry in Canada today. He promised me that if I refrained from telling him about his business, he would not tell me how to write narrative verse. His name was Rodger Touchie, and he is the publisher of this book.

We set out to produce and publish a volume of poetry, but thematically it soon became a nightmare because the collection of "stuff" I had was such a formless potpourri, ranging from traditional narrative verse through blank verse and *vers libre* to the Scots verse form of Robert Burns, the ancient Celtic/British ballad form, limericks, and parodies of famous poetic works and lyrics, some of them scurrilous. Rodger observed that my passion for narrative verse, combined with my exposure to many and varied Canadian social, political and historic events, had given me a voice—his choice of word—that younger Canadians ought to be able to hear. So we culled the collection and began to concentrate on recognizably Canadian material that had been inspired by some of the "wows" I had expressed since coming to Canada.

The title was chosen because one of our heroes—both Rodger's and mine—was a seminal figure in the emergence of western Canada as we know it today: the legendary Sam Steele of the North West Mounted Police. There is a famous photograph of a long string of gold-hungry miners hauling themselves hand over hand up the precipitous Chilcoot Pass in Alaska in the 1890s, on their way toward the Yukon gold diggings. They reached the summit in single file, and there they found Sam Steele, waiting to welcome them to Canada in the name of the Queen and her Mounted Police and to relieve them, one at a time, of their firearms, which were illegal in Canada.

Steele first came west, as a teenaged soldier, to help quell the Red River Rebellion in 1870 and returned as an officer when the Mounties made their great march west in 1873. Early in the 20th century, he wrote his only book, which he called *Forty Years in Canada*. We reckoned if it was a good enough title for Sam's book, it would fit mine, too.

Reading about characters like Sam Steele and Colonel James Macleod and the hardy souls who crossed the Atlantic has always made me wonder what it must have been like to arrive in this country 200 years ago, not so much as an immigrant as a castaway, for that was how the first Scots arrived in this land, and they had no idea what awaited them or how they might be able to survive. They knew only that they had been uprooted and evicted from their ancestral homes, and that the future stretching ahead of them was nothing if not bleak.

Bill McKinney never read my poem "The Song of the Exile" because in those days I showed no one my poetry, and I would not publish my first novel for seven more years, but he would have smiled and nodded, sucking on his pipe, to read the end of it, wondering if his own ancestors could ever have foreseen a descendant who would one day be honoured as the colonel of a hallowed Canadian regiment.

So here we go. The poems appear exactly as I wrote them, and, as you will already have guessed, I have made only a partial attempt to create a linear flow of experiences and memories. My home base for the past four decades has been western Canada, and because some of my fondest memories are linked to geographic locations, I organized much of the verse in this book into chapters about particular western provinces. Because the Royal Canadian Legion and the veterans I came to know in my early days in Alberta made such an impression on me, I have included a chapter on them, and on the importance of remembering people and events, and it ties in rather neatly to the brief section of reminiscences dealing with my days as the regimental bard of the Calgary Highlanders and of the Calgary Burns Club.

And then, of course, there's the wee bit about being a writer. I couldn't get away with not dealing with that topic. I did not touch upon the difference between being a writer and being a poet, however, for I have no idea how to deal with it—at least, not at this point. I still write narrative verse from time to time, but the challenge of writing hefty historical novels to tight deadlines tends not to leave much room for sitting around struggling with rhymes and verse.

Jack Whyte
Kelowna, BC
August 2007

The Song of the Exile

Cast off the anchor and unfurl the sail,
Drown the cry of the gull in the pibroch's sad wail.
Farewell to our mountains, adieu to our glen,
We, her children, will never see Scotland again,
For we're bound o'er the ocean, cast off on the deep,
Our land taken from us to feed England's sheep.
We're sentenced and outcast; condemned, dispossessed,
Torn away from our homeland and shipped to the West.

We are lost now, and frightened, cut off from our dreams,
From our mountains and moor lands and swift-running streams;
From our loved ones and families, our proud Celtic past,
Cast adrift on the ocean, to settle at last
In some country unsettled and savage and wild,
Where we'll have to build shelter for mother and child
From the wind and the weather, the frost and the snow.
God, grant us the strength to stand tall where we go!

There's a land men call Canada, somewhere out there,
With a beauty, they tell me, no man can compare.
But will we be able to carve out our mark
In a country whose history is shrouded in dark?
How far must we wander? How far must we roam?
How long will it take us to build a new home?
Will this Canada let us grow strong and stand free?
Dear God, that's in Thy future, for no man to see.

CHAPTER ONE

EARLY DAYS: ATHABASCA

I find it hard to believe that four decades have elapsed since I first set foot in Canada, and looking back now at the goggle-eyed naïf who was me, I also find it hard to believe how unworldly and sublimely confident I was at the age of 27, setting out to find a brand-new life in a country about which I knew absolutely nothing. It seemed like an advanced age in those days, but now I can see just how young and raw I really was. The depth and extent of my ignorance is crystallized for me by events that I can still clearly recall from the afternoon of July 13, 1967, my first day in Canada.

We arrived in Alberta at Edmonton International Airport on a beautiful sunny afternoon, after nine hours in the air on the transpolar flight from Heathrow Airport in London—my wife, Helena, myself and our two children, Jeanne, aged six, and Michael, who was four. We were met by an emissary from the board of trustees (colloquially, the School Board) of the County of Athabasca #12, and I was amazed at how many miles it was, through flat, empty fields, from Edmonton International Airport to the southern boundary of the city.

Edmonton was a low-lying kind of place in those days, with an air of great spaciousness and a lack of stress. There were several impressive high-rises in the downtown core, but very few buildings beyond the core were even three or four storeys high. Edmonton struck me as being a city of wide streets and small houses on well-treed, spacious lots. On the outskirts of the city, a replica of the Leduc #1 derrick, the first oil-pumping well in the region, announces to everyone that Edmonton is the oil capital of Canada. The first time I saw that sign, which was on the way in from the airport on my first day in Canada, I of course had no idea that there was rivalry between Edmonton and Calgary over that apparently innocuous claim.

Edmonton, as our escort proudly told us that day, was also the provincial capital, boasting a fine set of formal Victorian-style parliament buildings overlooking the deeply cut North Saskatchewan River valley. Looking out at the city from the heights of the High Level Bridge that day, though, one would have seen absolutely no hint of how much the city was to grow in the coming decades.

Strangely enough, although I can clearly recall being taken to see the Legislative Buildings, which seemed oddly small and foreshortened, somehow, after my years of living in and around London and its massive piles, I really recall nothing about my first sighting of Edmonton itself. But an hour and a half later, as we were barrelling north up Highway 2 and nearing the township of Westlake, en route to the town of Athabasca and my first Canadian teaching post, I saw something I had never seen before. Off to my right was a large rooster tail of dust billowing up from the ground and spiralling skyward. It appeared to be moving north just as quickly as we were. I was mystified. I asked our driver what it was, and he looked out his window, clearly expecting to see something unusual and frowning slightly when he didn't. He asked me to be more specific, and when he finally focused on what had intrigued me, he shrugged and looked vaguely disappointed. It was probably a half-ton, he told me, driving along a gravel road that paralleled the highway.

I had no idea what he was talking about. I had never heard of a "half-ton" and had never seen a gravel road—in fact, I had never even *heard* of gravel roads. But once I understood his answer, I understood another enigma that had been niggling at me for months. In the literature I had received from my new employer (known simply at that time as the County of Athabasca #12), a great deal had been made of the fact that the town of Athabasca lay 90-some miles north of the city of Edmonton and that all but seven miles of the road connecting the two places were paved. I had been wondering exactly what this meant, because in western Europe and the UK, where I had spent my whole life up until then, *all* roads are paved. They have been there for a long time, and it is inconceivable to a European that a major road might not be paved. Yet here was clear and incontrovertible evidence that in western Canada, they had not yet had time to pave all the roads. This was my introduction to the reality of how new, compared with Europe, and largely unused western Canada was. The house in Scotland in which I grew up is more than 200 years old; the city of Calgary, which would become important to me later, would not celebrate its 100th birthday until eight years after I'd arrived in Athabasca.

Soon after that, I recognized an even greater difference between worlds old and new: the gulf between people's perceptions of distance. I grew up less than 20 miles southeast of Glasgow, and although my mother's family lived only 15 miles southwest of it, we seldom visited them. It was a long way, and it involved going into the city and changing buses. Within three months of coming to Canada, I wrote home in all innocence that we thought nothing of piling the kids and their sleeping bags into the station wagon on a Friday evening and driving 90 miles south to a drive-in movie, then another 90 miles home again. My siblings at home were all shocked, incapable of imagining such a trek. And, of course, that perception has its mirror opposite here in Canada.

Case in point: I was telling my class one day about the Battle of Bannockburn, fought in AD 1314, when I noticed one of the "cool" students—a kid called Carl Bernard—sneering openly at what I was saying. It was a real Elvis Presley sneer, and when I called him on it, he scoffed and asked me what kind of fools I took them for. I was always talking about these battles, he said, and pretending I'd been to all the battlefields even though it was plainly impossible to have done such a thing. Young Carl was no dummy; he just couldn't absorb the truth about distances in Britain. And the truth is, there is a belt of land perhaps 10 miles wide, close to the ancient town of Stirling, that is the gateway to the Scottish Highlands. Its proper name is the Carse of Stirling, and every invading army that ever marched into Scotland from England has had to negotiate that strip of land, and it's where the opposing, defending Scots waited for them. Thus a huge number of the great battles in Scotland's history have been fought within a few miles of each other, but hundreds of years apart. Born and raised in that area, I would visit all of these battlefields many times in my boyhood, mostly on foot; occasionally, I had visited a couple of sites in the same morning or afternoon. My Canadian students simply could not visualize that, because Canada is so young and so vast, and towns and villages so far apart.

There was a large black-and-white map of Alberta in the school where I taught that first year. It featured a pattern of squares and made no sense to me until I received a lesson in civics and geography from one of my teaching colleagues, Frank Appleby, who would later leave teaching to go into provincial politics. Frank briefly explained how surveyors had split up the enormous land into ranges and townships. On my first trip by air from Edmonton to Calgary, I looked out the window and sure enough, there it was below me, the entire landscape laid out in flawless squares, just like the squares on that old map.

When I think about such things now, I tend to shrug my shoulders mentally and change gears, but I have come to believe that my early impressions of Canada were seminal. Everything was so new and striking, and I was so enthusiastic and impressionable, that these powerful images and memories are still with me, registered indelibly on my awareness.

The timing of my arrival, in July of 1967, could not have been better. It was the centennial of Confederation, and Canada was at its apogee. The words of Wilfrid Laurier, to the effect that the 20th century belonged to Canada, still seemed appropriate and accurate: it would be another decade and a half, in the early 1980s, before people would begin to question that perception. To be a Canadian in July 1967 was to have the world at your command. Yours was the second-largest and the most resource-filled country in the world, with a standard of living and a self-esteem that were second to none. Nothing seemed impossible, and Canada appeared invincible in every direction and from every perspective. Charles de Gaulle had not yet uttered his infamous exhortation *"Vive le Quebec libre,"* and Pierre Trudeau had not yet said "Just watch me" as he invoked the War Measures Act.

Not that either of those events alone ended the idyll Canada was enjoying, but each of those incidents, in its own way, marked an end and a beginning for me as an observer. De Gaulle's declaration, and his immediate expulsion from Canada thereafter, was the first sign I had that not everything was perfect in Canada, and Trudeau's invocation of the War Measures Act was an overt demonstration of power unmatched by anything I had ever seen in the United Kingdom.

Those initial impressions eventually inspired me to write "On Being Canadian," my first poem about Canada, some time in 1968 or '69. It was a simple piece, composed of the rhyming couplets so beloved of Alexander Pope, but written in iambic heptameter, a rhythm I thought at the time was different and noteworthy enough for the piece I had in mind. It was sincere and heartfelt, if naive, and I had no idea it was to be the first of many poems I would write about the fascinating and exciting land in which I now lived. Although I updated it years later, mainly because I felt I could improve upon it, it remains largely unchanged, merely expanded.

On Being Canadian
As an Immigrant, I landed here in nineteen sixty seven
And I thought that, leaving Britain, I had flown non-stop to Heaven.
It was Canada's Centennial and everywhere I saw
People celebrating Canada; their land, their life, their Law.

I found a new world, shining bright and full of smiling pride;
Where fortunes waited to be made and men felt good inside;
I found a place where men and women, immigrants like me,
Sang out in celebration of their True North, strong and free.

I found a place where people stood together, hand in hand,
And took delight in singing of their home and native land;
All glowing with the knowledge that, no matter whence they'd come,
They were here, alive, in Canada, in freedom and in sum!

I'd found a place where people's names fell, just the slightest bit
Like a roll of alien nations on the eardrums of a Brit;
Polish, German and Ukrainian, Danish, Dutch and Japanese,
And yet each one was Canadian, not just Scotch, French or Chinese!

I remember the excitement that I felt when I found out
That standing tall and being You was what life was about
In this new world men called Canada, this mighty, massive land

That was honoured and respected, and my awe was huge and grand.

Then, that summer, Charles De Gaulle raised up his voice for 'Free Québec'
And I saw a part of wonderland go crashing into wreck
As Trudeau proclaimed War Measures and the FLQ ran wild
Yelling slogans and performing like a spoiled, wilful child.

I remember, too, 'though, one more night; the night I realized
That Canadians had something else that none even surmised,
When the Premier of Alberta left a dinner that they'd thrown
In his honour, and His Honour just walked out of there, alone!

No armed escort; no policemen; no security at all;
He was just a private citizen, going home after a Ball
With no thought of armed assassins ever coming to his mind,
Yet a Head Of State, for all that, and unique among his kind!

Here, I thought, was Revelation! and the notion came to me
That this land had far more freedom than the famed Home of the Free;
And I looked around the faces of my friends there, in that hall
And I thought, "God! They don't know it! They just can't see it at all!"

Nowadays, we've gone bilingual, and all multicultural, too;
The Canadian Identity's a problem through and through;
We're perplexed and we're frustrated; we're bewildered, unresigned
To a future we can't fathom, and we feel we're flying blind.

Disillusioned with our leaders at all levels yet again,
We're consumed with the inequities between women and men;
We're afraid for the environment; confused about Meech Lake;
The mystifying GST and how Free Trade will break;

We complain we don't know who we are, or who we might not be;
And we're worried that the government might kill the CBC;
And we've lost sight of the one great thing that's really all our own:
We're Canadian, goddammit! We should be ashamed to moan!

The town of Athabasca lies in the valley of the Athabasca River, which rolls right past it. Originally called Athabasca Landing, the town was the embarkation point for miners being lured north by the Yukon gold rush. They would board riverboats, barges or large canoes at the Landing, make their way downstream to the mighty Mackenzie River, and then fight their way upstream to where they would set off on foot for the Klondike, crossing mountain passes en route. In those days, before the gold rush fizzled out and the river traffic vanished almost overnight, there was talk of making Athabasca, with its 50,000-strong population, the capital of Alberta. When all but a thousand of those residents had vanished with the gold dust, political emphasis shifted toward Calgary and Edmonton, and the people left in Athabasca settled down to deal with the realities of living in a small Canadian town.

And what a town it was! I don't think I could have found a better place to experience my first Canadian year, because it encapsulated everything I had imagined about Canada as a boy, with closely packed evergreen trees encroaching upon the town outskirts, immensely wide streets in which a teamster could easily turn an eight-horse team if necessary, and the wide, wild Athabasca River flowing majestically at the foot of the main streets, offering promises of gold nuggets and swift passage to the not-too-distant lands of the Yukon.

Admittedly, most of my imaginings had been inspired by tales of the Great Canadian North from Jack London and Robert W. Service, but my first Canadian winter, especially the day when the temperature dropped to -36 degrees Fahrenheit, proved beyond a doubt that we were not in Britain anymore. I had walked across the street to Richards' hardware store that morning, to scrounge a ride up the hill to the school, which was about a mile and a half away from the teacherage (one of the many words I had never heard before coming to Canada). I was astonished to see everyone in the store buried up to their eyebrows in great down-filled parkas with fur-lined hoods. I stopped short inside the doorway and gaped at them all in surprise, and was completely mystified when they broke out in a concert of guffaws and hoots and hollers, staggering about and pointing at me and hugging themselves in paroxysms of mirth.

I had known it was cold that morning, so I'd gone back inside before leaving home and changed into my heavy-duty three-piece suit of Harris tweed, and that's what I was wearing when I walked into the store—a three-piece tweed suit with a shirt and tie. No coat. Sure, it was nippy, but I'd walked briskly across the street, carrying my briefcase, and it hadn't seemed *too* bad . . . It was only when they told me that it was 36 below out there that the cold hit me, and then it seemed to grow from the inside and radiate outwards. Prior to that morning, having spent my entire life in Britain and France, I had never experienced anything as cold as zero Fahrenheit, let alone 35 below.

But on July 13, 1967, that cold snap was still months ahead in a future I could not have imagined. From the moment we drove into town that first day, I was absorbing images that have stayed with me to this day. Primary among them is the old false-fronted livery stable with its faded, weathered legend that told me it had been established in the 1860s, at the time of the American Civil War and before Sam Steele and the Mounties had ever reached Fort Edmonton. Then there were the towering grain elevators down by the railway tracks; the sawmill where I would work on the green line until the school year started; and the Athabasca Hotel, in which we spent our first night and which had a bathtub with the most shallow sides I had ever seen—they couldn't have been more than a foot high.

The Athabasca Hotel sat at the lower end of town, right down toward the riverbank. You couldn't see the river from the hotel, but you could smell it on a summer's afternoon, and when you walked to where you could see it, you were impressed by the sheer volume of water surging along the channel. The forest pushed right up against the edge of town, evergreen trees shoulder to shoulder, so dense that they barely shed snow in the winter. You could be out of sight and sound of human habitation within minutes of leaving your doorstep. I saw my first moose there, not 15 minutes from my home, and I saw an enormous and skinny wolf in the same area of woodlands on a beautiful September evening after school.

Coffee—really good, strong coffee—was 10 cents a cup, with endless refills, and I ate a salad of iceberg lettuce for the first time in my life. I couldn't believe how crisp and solid it was—lettuce that actually crunched between your teeth! The only lettuce we had ever seen or eaten in Britain back then was the kind Canadians call butter lettuce, and we had only ever had one salad dressing, a gooey, repulsive mayonnaise concoction bottled by Crosse & Blackwell.

It was in the sawmill that I got my introduction to Canadian humour. I had six weeks to kill between my arrival in town and the start of the school year, and Richard Hall, my cordial landlord, suggested that I might enjoy finding a job and meeting some of the people among whom I would be living from then on. He said he would put in a word for me with the owner of the local sawmill, and sure enough, I started work the following Monday morning.

It was high summer, and as I walked the half-mile or so between where I lived and the sawmill, which was sprawled along the riverbank, I would revel in the *differentness* of everything around me. The dust along the dirt entrance road was like talcum powder, and I could smell its dryness as I trudged through it, aware of the way it lay half an inch thick on the plants that lined the roadside and exploded outwards from my feet with every step. On my right, between me and the river, tall grasses and thick reeds hemmed me in so that I could see nothing but what lay ahead of me: the board fences and shingled roofs of the sawmill.

My employer gave me a brand-new pair of leather work gloves and put me to work on the green line, and for the next month I was steeped in the smells of sawdust, resin and newly cut lumber—and more than a little deaf from the incessant noise. Of course, I didn't even know what a green line was—it's the system of tables and rollers on which raw "green" lumber is fed into the band saw to be cut into planks. The only thing I'd seen that was remotely like the huge industrial band saw the green line serviced was a tiny cousin with a quarter-inch blade, mounted on a bench in the woodworking shop in my boys' school in Scotland. But the band saw in the Athabasca sawmill was an impressive affair with a revolving, changeable blade that could be six or more inches in depth and that would slice a two-foot-thick hemlock log into planks as easily as a hot knife cutting butter.

My job was to stand at the end of the green line and collect the emerging pairs of two-by-eight-inch, eight-foot-long planks delivered to me by Max, an enormous Cree man who fed the lumber into the saw as single 4½ x 8-inch, eight-foot lengths. I learned quickly how to stand properly as I waited for the newly cut planks to come off the rollers so that I could grasp the pairs at the midpoint and hump them about three paces across the floor to pile them where someone else would feed them into the planer—the loudest mechanical device I had ever encountered. (And only now, in writing about it, have I become aware that absolutely no one in that entire place wore ear protectors or safety goggles of any kind.) This was, of course, in the days before computerized automation, which revolutionized sawmills and every other conceivable kind of mill. All the donkey work in the mill was done by hand, by manpower, and the top man in my section of the operation, the green line, was Big Max.

Max intimidated me, and he knew it. I had never met a genuine Indian before—they wouldn't become known as First Nations for a while yet—and I had never expected them to be so *big*. Max was huge, and for days he glared at me balefully each time I met his eyes. Most of the time he kept his head down and just sliced big planks into smaller planks, all day, every day, neither speaking to me nor smiling, refusing to acknowledge my existence in any way. And I, of course, just off the boat, still wet behind the ears and completely lacking in confidence and assertiveness, accepted that as being normal behaviour. Until the day they changed the feed.

I had noticed *something* different that morning, but I could not have told you what it was—I suppose it was a slight, attitudinal change in the guys on the crew. I sensed that there was something going on, but I had no clue as to what it was, and it didn't cross my mind that it might have something to do with me. Anyway, they had changed the blade on the saw and they told me we would be processing bigger planks that day, twelve-foot-long 2 x 12s instead of eight-foot-long 2 x 8s. I would have to adjust my grip to accommodate the broader width and increased weight of the planks, they said, but the basic technique was pretty much the same as before: hoist the load off the rollers, hitch it up onto one hip, then walk it to the pile. Big Max switched on the saw. And then all hell broke loose.

The first pair of planks came along the rollers and I grasped it, gauging the new hoist point accurately enough, then yarded it up onto my hip. And there my world seemed to crash to an end. My colleagues had told me what was different, but they hadn't explained what would actually *happen*. I had captured the knack of balancing the eight-foot planks on my hip, but carrying the 12-footers was a whole new game. The extra two feet made each end of the planks sag, and they smacked against the floor on either side of me, rebounded violently to smack against each other like clappers, then smacked against the floor again. I felt exactly like the cartoon character Wile E. Coyote, stunned, rattled and jarred into terror. As I went into shock, Big Max slammed his hand against the OFF switch to stop the band saw and leaped at me, wide-eyed and roaring, his arms high up above his head.

I aged about five years in 10 seconds, scared out of my wits until I realized that all the guys on the crew, including Max, were reeling around helplessly, hugging their middles, weak-kneed from the draining effects of their demented laughter, which lasted for the remainder of that day, re-emerging from time to time as fits of giggles. Of course I had been set up, as was every single newbie who went to work there. The subtle thing I had noticed earlier had been their anticipation of what they were going to do to me, and every one of them had been in on it. But that was the end of Max's silence and lack of smiles. I was accepted. That same afternoon, he gave me an envelope containing a single, brand-new, unfolded centennial-year dollar bill. He told me not to spend it, that there would never be another one quite like it because Canada would never have another 100th birthday, and that I should keep it as a souvenir of my first job. I still have it.

That centennial year was more amazing and probably far more meaningful to me and other impressionable and incredulous recent immigrants than it was for most Canadian-born adults, who, being Canadian, saw it as little different from the years that had preceded it and were appropriately self-effacing and phlegmatic about the whole thing. They were certainly visibly proud of what they had going for them, but to a great extent they were inured to having the good times flow around and over them, and thus simply took the bounty of Canadianism for granted. After all, it had been developing for 100 years. To us, the newcomers from other less enlightened and less optimistic societies, Canada was astoundingly new and viscerally exciting, and the centennial year in which we found ourselves immersed was quite literally the first year of the rest of our lives. And for me, at least, it was filled with experiences, observations and insights that affected me deeply and have shaped my thinking on a wide range of issues ever since.

In the movie theatre below the teacherage that was our first home, the entire audience stood up and sang the national anthem every night, and I never grew tired of watching and marvelling at that. In Britain, the opening notes of the national anthem would invariably signal a stampede for the nearest bus stop. In Canada in 1967, it was different. People stood up proudly and vaunted their Canadianism; at the hint of an invitation, they would detail their Canadian ancestry, right back to the day when their immigrant ancestors stepped off the boat, and yet they still spoke of themselves in those days as Ukrainians, Germans, Poles, Russians, Brits and the like, putting their ethnic nationality ahead of their Canadian one.

Westerners

Did your ancestors pioneer this ground?
Can you trace your descent that far back?
Are you proud of your family background,
Of their success, despite what they lacked?
Well, remember, my friend, when you're tempted
To turn up your nose at hard work,
That the price of this land they pre-empted
Was sweat, by the gallon, and work.

And remember, too, friend, when you wrinkle
Your nose at a "manual" job,
That you wouldn't be able to crinkle
Your brow had gran'paw been a snob:
If those people had clamoured for Welfare
And socialised medicine and care,
This country could not have grown healthy
And you would be—I wonder? Where?

Yes, it's strange when you think of the drifters
Who first made this country their home,
The con-men, the hookers, the grifters
Who left the big cities to roam;
Of the miners, the ranchers, the settlers,
The outcasts, the misfits, the fools
And the gamblers who took a new country
And made it conform to new rules.

For this land that we all take for granted
Was constructed by men wild and rough
At a time when you took what you wanted,
And if you couldn't handle it—tough!
For theirs was the law of the jungle
Where only the strong stayed alive
And the quitter who hollered out "Uncle"
Was a creature who couldn't survive.

Look around you, my friend, and remember
That this West's just a hundred years old,
That the ground won't produce in December
And a man has to battle the cold
Every bone-chilling day for a half-year
And sleep warm every long winter night,
And be honest, my friend, could you stay here
Had those ancestors not won their fight?

I used to visit the theatre's projection room every night to shoot the breeze with Richard Hall, the theatre owner and projectionist and also my landlord. I saw every movie that played in town from midsummer to midwinter that year, and I enjoyed hours of wide-ranging conversation with Richard during the subsequent showings of the movies I'd seen. He was a fountain of information about Canada and Alberta, a fascinating man who had done many things in his long life, and done most of them well. I was still sufficiently young and impressionable at 27 to be awed by his experience, insight and imperturbable urbanity.

I will never forget the night he came to our apartment for coffee and to look at the new paint job my wife and I had just given the living room: peach-coloured walls with white woodwork and trim. He and I had just watched *The War Wagon* that night, starring John Wayne and Kirk Douglas—I remember that clearly because the reels were out of order, and we showed the end of the movie before the middle. It was early October, and it would have been between 10:30 and 11 o'clock. The theatre had just emptied and I had helped him lock up and stack the reel cases for collection the next morning.

As I poured coffee, Richard surveyed our living room. My grandfather's old Westminster chimes clock stood on the mantel over the fireplace, and Richard looked from it to the bookshelves that held our 12-volume set of the Child ballads, the celebrated collection of old British songs that is generally regarded as the canon of folk music, and which I had been given as a parting gift upon leaving the folk club I had founded in England.

Richard wrinkled his nose and pushed his glasses up higher, then peered at the old double-sashed windows that overlooked the theatre marquee and the main street. He told me then, apropos of nothing, that if ever we needed to get out of there, I should open the window and climb out onto the marquee with my family, then close the window behind us. If the window jammed, he said, I should smash it out with a wooden chair. I smiled and nodded and said I would.

About a month later, new machines were installed in the concessions booth. Helena and I awoke in the middle of a raw wintry night to a barrage of noises from downstairs that sounded exactly like the racket we used to make as kids when we ran along an iron fence, dragging sticks against the metal palings. It turned out that what we were hearing was the sound of concession-booth pop cans exploding in the heat of the fire burning in the theatre downstairs. I called the fire department, and when the chief, who answered the phone himself, asked me how bad it was, I looked down and saw that the linoleum on the kitchen floor beneath my feet was bubbling. When I told him that, he instructed me in one short, pithy sentence to leave immediately.

We dressed ourselves and the children completely and clambered out onto the marquee. I still can't believe how calm I was throughout it all, even remembering to slip my wallet into the inside pocket of my suit (with Max's dollar bill). A short time later, wrapped in blankets and watching from the deck of a truck on the other side of the street, we saw the smoke magically clear from our living room just moments before my grandfather's prized clock exploded into flames on the mantel. (For years after that, every time he saw a fire truck, my son Michael, who was four at the time, would whisper to me, "Daddy, dem mans burned our house.")

We were young, we had no money saved, and the few possessions we had had were uninsured. I had been teaching in the high school for less than a semester; we were still strangers to the town. Now, overnight, we had been made destitute, and I was frantic. But I was about to receive my most memorable lesson on the way things work in Canada, in small, rural towns like Athabasca. To my amazement, before noon the day after the fire we had a new apartment in which to live, and the people of the town and the surrounding areas—people we had never met or heard of—had begun rallying to support us. The following week was easily and beyond question the most astonishing time of my life, as help and support were showered upon us from all directions in a spirit of goodwill and unadulterated altruism that still influences me today whenever I find myself dealing with people less fortunate than I am.

CHAPTER TWO

REMEMBERING

As a result of the fire and our subsequent surge in popularity, getting to know our neighbours in a short length of time, I found myself spending a fair number of winter evenings at the local branch of the Royal Canadian Legion, because that was where Athabascans went to socialize in 1967. There, a mere 22 years after the Second World War ended, I met many men and women who had actually fought to make Canada what it had become, and they were all still relatively young.

I was not a drinker—I didn't even like the taste of beer in those days—but I enjoyed sitting in the members' lounge and listening to the stories and to the debates, some of which had been argued, pro and con, for years. One such discussion led to my tackling my second Canadian poem. It started out specifically to be free verse, I remember, because I really wanted to capture the conflicting viewpoints that had excited me that night, and free verse seemed to offer a convenient and versatile medium in which to achieve that, but soon after I started writing I got bogged down in the philosophical elements of the debate, which is usually a pretty good sign, I have found, that you won't be able to say what you want to say with any kind of clarity.

The debate was triggered by the flag that had been hoisted that very day outside the Legion hall to replace the one that had been shredded in a high wind some time earlier. Some of the fellows were talking about it later over a few beer, served in tiny glasses on petite orange-terry-covered tables, and before long they were getting pretty specific, comparing the "new" flag, the red and white Maple Leaf, to the "old" one, the Canadian Red Ensign, and detailing the pros and cons of each.

It seems strange to think of it now, but in 1967 the Maple Leaf flag was only two years old. It had been unveiled in February 1965 by then-prime minister Lester B. Pearson, and to say that not everyone in Canada was convinced it was the right emblem for the country would be stating the case mildly, especially in the western provinces, where there are relatively few maple trees to be seen.

This much was evident by the discussion in Athabasca that night. Remembrance Day was approaching, and a surprising number of the veterans, anticipating their third cenotaph ceremony with Canada's new standard, still felt that the flag was lacking in tradition, history and associated sacrifice. Of course, someone *did* say that this would change, given a little time, but at that moment, as everyone turned to look at the old Red Ensign in its dusty glass-fronted case on the wall, few were willing to concede that that person might be right—which, of course, he was.

When I tried a second time, a decade or so later, to write about that night, it emerged as a song, "The Old Dominion Red," which I have sung in many, many different Legions. But I never did sing it in Athabasca, and all the vets I can remember who were there that night are now dead.

The Old Dominion Red

It was on a night, oh, years ago,
The local Legion threw an old-time dance;

The band was so-so, as bands go, and all the vets
Were tripping back to France.
The beer and tears were flowing
As the band played "Bless 'Em All" and "London Pride"
And they talked about how time had flown,
And thought about the friends they'd known,
And how they'd marched together, side by side.

>   And over in the corner by the portrait
>   Of Her Majesty The Queen,
>   Stood the white and scarlet Maple Leaf,
>   Where once the old Dominion flag had been.
>   It was bright and it was pretty,
>   But like one old-timer sitting near me said,
>   Nobody there had fought for it;
>   No victories had been bought for it;
>   The vets had known the Old Dominion Red.

Someone sang of blue birds over
The old chalky cliffs of Dover far away,
But he forgot the words and stumbled in his singing
And what more was there to say?
And among the younger people there, heads shook
And there were some embarrassed smiles
Because they couldn't understand
How folks could get so out of hand
And cry about forgotten wars and styles.

>   And over in the corner by the portrait
>   Of Her Majesty The Queen,
>   Stood the white and scarlet Maple Leaf,
>   Where once the old Dominion flag had been.
>   It was bright and it was pretty,
>   But like one old-timer sitting near me said,
>   Nobody there had fought for it;
>   No victories had been bought for it;
>   The vets had known the Old Dominion Red.

Well, I remember feeling rotten
As I looked around that noisy, smoke-filled hall

For there, dusty and forgotten,
I could see the old flag hanging on the wall;
But I had never seen it flapping in its glory
In the old, blood-stirring way,
And I had no cause to remember
The Eleventh of November
As being different from any other day.
    And yet, over in the corner by the portrait
    Of Her Majesty The Queen,
    Stood the white and scarlet Maple Leaf,
    Where once the old Dominion flag had been.
    Sure, it was bright and it was pretty,
    But like that old fellow sitting there had said,
    Nobody there had fought for it;
    No victories had been bought for it;
    The vets had known the Old Dominion Red

In the late 1960s, the Second World War and the Korean War were still recent enough memories that many people in their late 40s and mid-50s could remember what it had actually meant to be "over there," and the Royal Canadian Legion was a thriving, going concern with genuine relevance to Canadians of that generation. Attrition over the decades has practically wiped out that generation, and the immediacy of their memories is being lost. The people who replaced them, who are now middle-aged themselves, have never known conflict on the scale their parents and grandparents knew, and only today, in the light of our ongoing losses in Afghanistan, are they beginning to gain some insight into what it means to lose loved ones in a war.

A tiny bit of Canadian history dies each time we hear or read of the death of another of the Canadians who served with distinction in those earlier conflicts. As I write this, the oldest surviving Canadian veteran of the First World War is 107 years old, living in Spokane,

Washington. He was too young to fight in the trenches, but he went over there in uniform, willing to fight and die for his beliefs if he was called upon. And now he is the last Canadian living who was there.

With every death among such veterans we come closer, unfortunately but inevitably, to the time when we as a people will have no real or relevant memory of those wars. And in the meantime, the ever-decreasing number of veterans has thrown many branches of the Royal Canadian Legion into crisis. After 60 years of relative peace and prosperity, the organization has quite literally run out of eligible candidates for membership and has consequently been obliged to seek creative ways of sustaining itself, extending membership to children, grandchildren and relatives of former members. And as the ranks of living veterans dwindle rapidly, there are barely enough young vets to maintain the organization.

Remember Them, Their Name is Legion

Remember them, their name is Legion;
They left their homes and went away
From every province, from every region,
And they left their kids this Canada
That we enjoy today.
Side by side, shoulder to shoulder,
They showed the world a rising star;
When, as young Canadian soldiers
They bore their country's flag to war.

When the news came that the world was plunged in conflict,
They came flocking from the forests and the fields,
From the islands, from the prairies, from the parklands,
From the Rockies and the great Laurentian Shield.
And they saw hell in Ypres town and Dieppe Harbour,
And they drowned in Passchendaele's devouring mud,

They took the Vimy Ridge and they were at the Arnhem Bridge
And the soil of Europe glutted on their blood.

So remember them, their name is Legion;
They left their homes and went away
From every province, from every region,
And they left their kids this Canada
That we enjoy today.

From Alberta, from Quebec and Nova Scotia,
From Saskatchewan, BC and Newfoundland,
From New Brunswick, PEI and Manitoba,
From Ontario and all the Northern Lands,
All the youth of Canada marched out for freedom
In their thousands, strong beneath the Maple Leaf,
And too many thousands died underneath a foreign sky
For their children's hopes and dreams and their beliefs.

Side by side, shoulder to shoulder,
They showed the world a rising star;
When, as young Canadian soldiers
They volunteered and went to war.
So remember them, their name is Legion;
They left their homes and went away
From every province, from every region,
And they left for us this Canada
That we enjoy today.

   As part of the last generation to have parents and family members
who were personally involved in the two so-called "great" world wars,
I have a soft spot for the veterans' associations, and I sympathize
deeply with their efforts to maintain their roles as repositories of the
memorabilia and records of the men and women who bore the brunt
of defending their nation and withstanding the forces being brought to
bear against them.

One of those men, and also one of the most unforgettable characters I ever met, was drum major of the pipe band of the General Stewart Branch of the Legion in Lethbridge, Alberta. The drum major in a pipe band is the most flamboyant character of all, strutting proudly and defiantly in full regalia at the head of the band, leading the way and dictating tempo and pace by means of the long staff—the mace—that is his badge of office. Archie MacFarlane, known to everyone in the Lethbridge and Alberta Scots communities as "Big Airch," was the quintessential drum major, and I first met him at the Lethbridge Rodeo Days in 1969, where I sang as one of the starring acts in the grandstand show. We spent several hours that weekend talking together in the convivial warmth of the General Stewart Branch, and it was the start of a friendship that lasted until Archie's death in 1990.

"Big Airch" was an enormous, florid-faced Scot with a magnificent, snowy white military moustache—the kind with its ends waxed and twisted into needle points—and a bearing, a natural dignity, that was absolutely regal. Even in his everyday clothes he was a giant of a man, but when he donned his full kilt and regalia he was stupendous and intimidating. Yet he was gentle and generous by nature, with a slight lisp and a soft-spoken voice that he seldom raised above a murmur when he wasn't on parade. He also was one of the last survivors of the contingent of the regiment known as the Kosbies, the King's Own Scottish Borderers, which was parachuted in to destroy the bridge at Arnhem, in Holland, in 1944 . . . the group that went, in the words of author Cornelius Ryan, "a bridge too far."

Archie came to Canada at the end of the war, settled in Lethbridge and never had any desire to move elsewhere after that. He joined the Legion on his arrival and, being a Scot and looking as impressive as he did, was invited to join the pipes and drums when the band was formed.

When he died, his funeral was remarkably well attended. My friend Morris MacFarlane, who had been general manager of that Legion branch for years, wrote a tribute to Archie and asked me if I would consider "tidying it up" for him. It was an honour and a privilege to do so, and I took great delight in being able to demonstrate and amplify the rhythmic tenor-drum rattle that Morris, despite his protestations of not being a poet, had managed to weave into the tribute to his friend and mine, Drum Major Archie MacFarlane.

Big Airch

When big Archie stepped forrit, oh man, he was grand,
In his braw feather bonnet and hackle;
He was Cock o' the North, at the head o' the band,
Starched and polished, an' rigid as spackle!

Aaron ance had a Rod; Moses wielded a Staff;
Archie gained his renown wi' a Mace;
And he swung it, by God, like a Ghillie his gaff,
Wi' distinction, precision and grace!

The auld tunes of glory were nectar to Arch
Their music put the braggart in his step;
He could tell a whole story in one short, Slow March
And you'd smell the smoke o' Arnhem and Dieppe.

Aye, and many's the time he led proud legionnaires
On occasions that would glorify their names,
As he showed them off brawly at Galas and Fairs
An' at Festivals, Parades and Highland Games.

There was only one Muirhead; one "Archie The Grand"
In this wee town, this Lethbridge o' ours;
Just one braw, perfect Drummie, the kind that could stand,
Sun or snaw, like a ramrod, for hours.

He's awa' now, ye ken, reunited wi' men
He once knew in his days as a KOSBIE.
The soldier's Valhalla will suit the old fella . . .
White wings, and a kilt, plaid and Busbie . . .

For he stood wi' the best, this grand man o' the West,
Among men o' high rank and proud Orders,
And his warm, gentle voice will mak' Heaven rejoice
Wi' its soft lowland lilt o' the Borders . . .

Jack's first publicity photograph, Calgary, about 1968

CHAPTER THREE

THE ENTERTAINER

When I left the UK in July 1967, I knew nothing about Alberta beyond the image I had been carrying in my mind for years. When I was 11, in 1951, my mother's sister Janette, my favourite aunt, left Scotland by sea for a new life in Canada. She ended up marrying a Scot, John Keane, whom she met on the boat, and settling down in Calgary, where John worked at the Esso Refinery. Every year after that, she sent home photographs of the Calgary Stampede parade, of the Indians decked out in their tribal finery, and the teepee village they set up on the Stampede grounds every year. It was heady stuff for a boy in Scotland who had hardly ever been outside the area in which he lived, and from the first time I saw those frilly-edged black-and-white snapshots, I swore to myself that I would go to Alberta one day and see it for myself. And then, in 1967, my opportunity came and I took it.

I had got married in 1964, while teaching in Brighton, on the south coast of England, and by 1966 I was the father of two children. For a number of reasons, primarily incompatibility, the marriage was not going well. But in those days, one did not simply turn around and get divorced—no one in my entire extended family had ever been divorced—so Helena and I decided to immigrate to Canada, in hopes that a complete change of environment might save our relationship.

Alberta needed teachers in the mid-1960s, and so I responded to an international advertisement in the *Times* Educational Supplement that touted the attractions of a life and career as a teacher in western Canada. The campaign worked spectacularly well, attracting a large number of young teachers to Alberta from the UK and Australia, many of them single, but most of them young married professionals with growing families, like me.

I have heard people say, "That's what made me the person I am today," in reference to some seminal event or junction in their lives, and when I look at my own life, I can say without hesitation or reservation that it was my experiences in Alberta, first in Edmonton in the late 1960s and most particularly in Calgary during the 1970s and the first half of the '80s, that shaped me into the person I have become. But the seminal event was my decision to quit the classroom and get out of the teaching profession.

It came about innocuously enough—or so it seemed at the time—while I was still teaching high school in Athabasca. I have had 40 years since then to think about what precipitated the end of my teaching career, and although I have never regretted moving on to other things, I am even more upset now than I was then about what happened to me and to scores, if not hundreds, of other young teachers at that time. I was one of the lucky ones, because I had sufficient natural talent to enable me to tell the self-styled authorities in the education business in 1968–69 to go fly a kite while I moved on to a career in music and entertainment.

The first sign that all was not as it appeared to be in the Elysian Fields of our new world as teachers in Alberta was that our credentials began to be questioned within months of our arrival. Of course, there was no cohesion amongst us at first—none of us was even aware that there were others like us. We had been scattered from the outset in schools throughout Alberta, and thus when we were taken to task for the perceived inefficacies of our qualifications, each of us took it personally and meekly assumed that "they"—the authorities and our employers—must be right and that we had somehow goofed in our course choices when we were students. Only later, as the school year went on and we began to encounter each other at various functions throughout the province, did we start comparing notes on our experiences as immigrants. Then it rapidly became clear that the universities in Britain, Europe and Australia, where we had acquired our qualifications, had been arbitrarily tried and found academically lacking compared to the standards of the University of Alberta in the 1960s. Of course, as soon as we understood this, we raised our eyebrows high in disbelief, because the universities in question were household names, worldwide.

A case in point: I had earned a *Diplôme d'études françaises* from the *Institut d'études françaises pour étudiants étrangers* in the city of Tours, in central France, which operated under the auspices of the Université de Poitiers, with distinction in French drama for producing, directing and acting in classical plays in the French language. It was deemed unacceptable and disallowed—which simply meant they no longer needed to pay me for it—because I had obtained it in France rather than at the university in Edmonton. The belief, plainly stated, was that I could have learned more about Molière and Jean-Paul Sartre had I studied them in Alberta rather than in France. And in the 1960s, Alberta ran rampant with anti-separatist attitudes and an entrenched belief, actually voiced to me on one occasion, that "we don't talk French in cattle country."

This, in a nutshell, was the kind of thing that hundreds of young teachers were being told and expected to swallow and accept. No education degree, be it from Oxford, London, Dublin/Trinity College, Queensland or any other university, was considered equivalent to a degree from the University of Alberta, which meant that we would have to "upgrade" our qualifications to Alberta specifications, at considerable personal cost.

Of course, what no one mentioned was that hiring several hundred new immigrant teachers, and then devaluing their qualifications after they had arrived, translated to hundreds of thousands of dollars in savings for education administrators all over Alberta. In my case, after almost five years' education in London and France, I was judged to be two English courses short of a basic bachelor's degree. This meant that I was paid for three and three-fifths years of training. Like other people in my circumstances, I had brought my family to Canada on an assisted-passage loan, which I had to repay, so I was already deeply in debt and would have faced a long swim back to Europe should I have wanted to register a protest.

It was a disgraceful and manipulative situation, and to this day it outrages me, but the apotheosis came when I was offered a "better" job in Edmonton. I had hosted the high school drama festival in Athabasca that year for the zone to which we belonged, and our entry, one of ten, won two of the three available trophies. Thus we went on to represent our zone in the provincial finals, where we won seven or eight out of thirteen trophies, one of them Best Director for me. As a direct result, I was offered the opportunity to head the brand-new drama department (a department of one, me) at McNally Composite High School, a newly built facility in the city of Edmonton. I was flattered and delighted— until I discovered what the ground rules were.

"The City of Edmonton School Board does not recognize partial increments," I was told in a tone of unctuous pomposity during the hiring interview.

"I'm not surprised," I thought. "I wouldn't either, not if they came leaping out of my breakfast cornflakes." Then I found out what that meant. Loosely translated, it went something like this: "You remember the three and three-fifths years of university we're paying you for? Well, we're cutting off the three-fifths of a year of pay because those are the aforementioned partial increments. And, uh, while we're on the topic of remuneration, you know those years of experience that enabled you to clean up in the drama festival? Well, see, you didn't gain that experience in Edmonton, so we're going to pro-rate you, and we'll pay you for only three years' experience, rather than for the years you've actually experienced, if you see what I mean. But smile, my friend. For the dubious and rapidly dwindling pleasure of coming to work for our bureaucracy, it's only going to cost you between 25 and 30 percent of your current, heavily pruned salary."

It was right about then that I told someone, very pointedly, where to go and what to do with his school system when he got there. It was difficult to swallow my fear and apprehension and make that decision, but I needed to break away from what I saw as an overwhelming agglomeration of petty, restrictive, bureaucratic bafflegab, the likes of which I had never encountered before. I was born at a time when people trusted the authorities, including their police forces, and still looked up to "professionals," who in turn were expected to govern themselves by ethical standards of conduct and behaviour, be they doctors, accountants, lawyers or schoolteachers. Now here I was, watching the start of the erosion that would undermine and finally destroy the classical educational standards against which I had measured myself.

People with innate teaching ability—that ineffable and indefinable but unmistakably magical spark that gives lasting and pleasurable memories of school days and moments of discovery to everyone lucky enough to experience it—were increasingly being sacrificed and rooted out in favour of so-called educators with specific academic credentials, the logic being that anyone with sufficient smarts to earn a Ph.D. in quantum mechanics or mathematics must be a brilliant, charismatic, resourceful teacher and a miraculous shaper of young minds.

This was the era when the appalling, indecipherable jargon used today by those involved in the "ed biz" was just starting to come into use. Parts of the gobbledygook "educators" were starting to spout so prolifically still resembled English at that time, but that was probably because the conventions of the jargon were too young and poorly formed to be self-sufficient at that stage. Nowadays, the claptrap they mouth and, God save us, set down on paper is utterly impenetrable to the uninitiated and untrained. I can imagine philologists of the future searching frantically for a Rosetta stone that will enable them to decipher the bureaucratic banalities of EdBizSpeak.

This was also the time when it was first being advocated, embraced and determined by—well, let's not get into by whom, for apparently no one ever really made such a decision; what happened occurred, apparently, as the result of a naturally occurring osmotic process. This is when it was being *decided*, in the passive voice and with italics, that there was really no need for students to learn the stultifying and difficult rules of spelling or grammar or punctuation as long as they could *communicate*.

It was also when the first guidance counsellors were being appointed in every school in the country, their ranks at that time consisting almost exclusively—because let's face it, it was a brand-new, formless, recently dreamed-up and consequently untested and effectively undefined profession—of disillusioned and frustrated teachers who felt less than comfortable actually teaching and attempting to maintain discipline in the classroom and therefore believed, in a knee-weakening triumph of illogical thinking, that they might be more effective if they channelled their self-perceived outstanding abilities toward *advising* the very students with whom they were uncomfortable.

And it was also the time when I became aware that here in Canada, hand in glove with what I perceived as appalling trends within the educational establishment, an astonishing and disconcerting number of working teachers viewed teaching itself only as an inconvenient but necessary hurdle to be overcome in the pursuit of a far more lucrative career in administration. Most Canadian-trained teachers wanted to get to that vice-principal's position, and from there gain an administrative posting as a bureaucrat within the education system. At times I wondered if some of them cared about the kids at all.

That's how I saw it then, and I haven't changed my mind, because the residue of all the disintegrative processes going on 40 years ago keeps popping back up to the surface of the slop bucket. Like the alarming discovery in the late '80s and early '90s that we were churning out university graduates whose written communication skills ranged from blank through semi-literate and all the way to functionally illiterate. A cry went up then for a return to the basics, but that's when we realized we couldn't go back to the basics, because all the young teachers in the business had been trained during the decades when the basics had fallen victim to the quest to *communicate*, and they themselves didn't know the basics.

So there I was in 1968, aware of the writing being graven on the wall, looking at the very fabric of my so-called profession and seeing little in it or about it that was admirable or inspiring. There were individual teachers with whom I had made friends (and I still remember them with fondness, although I have no idea where they are now), but beyond those well-remembered front-line faces I could see nothing engaging in either the teaching profession or the entire education field. As far as I could tell—and by that stage I was looking at things quite critically—with the marked and admirable exception of some of the teachers with whom I had taught, no one in the ranks of the administration with which I had been dealing possessed an ounce of genuine *passion* for what they did. No one cared enough to get excited or fired up about anything. And marching in lockstep with that lack of passion was a frightening lack of humour. I had had enough. In the brief space of one scholastic year I had been thoroughly, completely and permanently disillusioned, all my starry-eyed immigrant's optimism engulfed and obliterated by the bureaucratic cynicism that was becoming more deeply entrenched in the education system with each passing day. I could identify nothing of discernible substance, nothing worth emulating. Shockingly little inspired any reaction in me at all, other than a regretful, disillusioned head shake.

It occurred to me only recently that that brief one- to two-year period was the only time in my adult life in which I wrote nothing. I do not have a single line of verse, lyric or piece of prose written during that time, which in itself is indicative of how disillusioned and miserable I was. I wanted to walk away from teaching, to leave it all to the bureaucrats in spite of knowing how they would deface and mar and cripple what was left, but I was afraid, because I had been brought up to believe that my profession was my *security*.

Forget the fact that it was insecurity, and the demoralizing terror it brought with it, that had me living in a paradox, and never mind that I could plainly see how I and others like me had been manipulated and cheated and betrayed (although the pundits in the education biz had better, more orotund and euphemistic words for what had been done to us). The question causing me so much grief was: if I were to walk away from the classroom, *where would I go?*

That question terrified and haunted me. I knew I could probably make a living singing professionally in bars, for I had been successful as a folksinger in the UK, but my God! There was no security in that. That wasn't a *profession*. I had been told time and time again by everyone who had taken the time to wag a warning finger under my nose, including my wife, Helena, that even to think about singing professionally was an exercise in feckless self-indulgence. And that was the reaction to *singing*, which would allow me to go out at night and come home later with money in my pockets. The possibility that I might earn my bread by *writing* never even came up.

Helena and I had, of course, brought our marital problems with us to Canada, ending up thousands of miles away from our families, with no one to turn to for help or advice—not that either one of us had ever been good about taking advice—and things had gone from bad to irretrievable. We had managed, miraculously, I sometimes thought, to hold things together for our year in Athabasca, but everything disintegrated in the maelstrom of moving to Edmonton and finding myself looking for a new line of work.

I thought about all of this throughout the spring and early summer of 1968, debating the pros and cons of every aspect of where I was in my life and what I needed to do. And at the end of it I went out and bought a new set of strings for my guitar and became, for all intents and purposes, a wandering minstrel.

In the years that followed, I was asked a thousand times about the duration and quality of my musical training, and it always made me smile to see the expression on people's faces when I told them I was—and I remain—musically illiterate. "You show me a key signature," I would say, "and I'll show you a blank expression." The simple truth is that I never took the time to learn to read music. All the training I have came out of my childhood.

I was born into a musical family. My father and mother met originally in Johnstone, Renfrewshire, when both of them belonged to the choir at St. Margaret's Catholic Church. My mother was a natural, wonderful contralto, and my father had a basso profundo that was just getting into gear when I hit my bottom register. He could sing a full half-octave deeper than I ever could, and I had a solid, meaty bass-baritone range.

I don't recall there being a time when I was not singing, even when I was a preschooler. Mrs. McMaster, my first-grade teacher, made a point of getting me to stand up every Friday afternoon in music class and sing "My Grandfather's Clock." But I never did think of myself as a particularly good singer . . . certainly not good enough to sing for a living. The very idea was ludicrous and would have made me a laughingstock in my home village.

During the war—I was raised in the early 1940s in a coal-mining village called Cleland, near the town of Motherwell in Scotland's Clyde Valley in Lanarkshire—we lived in a state of blackout, with not the slightest glimmer of light being permitted to spill from the heavy blackout curtains after dark lest it attract the attention of an errant German bomber pilot cruising around at 10,000 feet, looking for a target on which to jettison his cargo of unused bombs. That seldom happened, but it was not altogether unheard of, and even toward the end of the war, the blackout rules were pretty solidly adhered to. But with nothing to do after dark every night except sit around at home, people soon began to make their own entertainment, and everybody, it seemed, was a singer.

Those were the *ceilidh* evenings, when friends and neighbours would gather together to while away the long winter nights. Sometimes someone would organize a concert or a recital or a play in the church hall—I saw J.M. Synge's wonderful Irish plays *The Playboy of the Western World* and *Riders to the Sea* performed there when I was only five or six years old. I was supposedly too young to understand what I was seeing, but Irish sentiment and tradition were so strong in our community that to this day I remember the atmosphere there in that old hall, and the plot details of the stories being told. And even then, I took it for granted that there were no non-Catholics in the crowd.

My paternal grandmother's people were Irish/Scots miners, which meant that they were Roman Catholic immigrants who had fled the potato famines of the previous century to serve as miners—virtual slave labourers in those days—in the Scottish coalfields. A hundred years later, when I was a boy, they were still regarded as second- or even third-class citizens, johnny-come-lately papist outsiders, regarded with generations-old distrust and dislike by the Presbyterian Scots among whom they had settled. So distinct and profound was the difference that I could tell, as a boy, a man's religion just by listening to him speak.

My Canadian friends accused me of exaggerating when I told them that, but it is the truth, easily illustrated with one simple question: "Are you going to church tomorrow morning?" That sentence is English, of course, so no one in our village would ever say it that way. A Catholic would put it, "Are yuh (or yiz) goin' to the chapel the morra mornin'?" His Protestant neighbour down the street would say, "Are ye gaun' tae the kirk, the mourn's mournin'?" Big difference, and a correspondingly big difference in attitudes.

But church-hall concerts were relatively rare and the appetite for entertainment among the people of our village insatiable, so every weekend, without fail, there were house parties that everyone attended. There was no overt drinking involved, although I suppose a few of the men didn't go for too long without having a bottle of beer or a dram of whisky, but such activities were always clandestine, and by and large these gatherings were teetotal affairs where the strongest beverage served was tea . . . *strong* tea, made in huge pots, with one heaping spoonful of loose black tea leaves thrown in for every person in attendance. There never was anything anemic about Scots-Irish tea. Because wartime food rationing was in force, the "meal" was freshly baked soda bread and butter, sometimes with homemade jam if the fruit harvest had been good, and at the end of it, in the old Irish Celtic tradition, everyone would draw their chairs up in a circle and the entertainment would begin.

Everyone had a party piece, either a song or a recitation, and was expected to perform it, no matter how many times the audience had heard it before and even if someone else had done it earlier. And no one ever interrupted the performances. It was considered the height of rudeness and a flagrant discourtesy to speak or whisper while someone was performing, irrespective of how boring or tone deaf the performer might be. Everyone had the right to be heard and to do his or her "bit" for the gathering.

My mother was a standout performer at these events, because she could sing any number of songs, whistle astonishingly well, with trills and fluting effects, and play the piano. So that's where I first learned to sing and perform, and it was never anything to grow conceited about. You stood up, you sang, and you sat down, and there were probably three or four other people in the room on any given night who could do everything better than you could.

When I was 11, I went to high school, which sounds bizarre to

Canadians nowadays, where high school starts at 14 or 15, but the explanation is simple. In Britain in those days, we all underwent an exam called the Eleven-Plus, which was part IQ and part language-skills testing, to determine whether we were most suited for an academic or a practical education. Those who were designated as academically apt were channelled into academic high schools, where they studied courses that would lead to university qualifications—the classics (Latin and Greek) and the standard sciences, mathematics, and languages. Those judged to be suitable for practical and trades training were admitted to junior high school, where they would graduate and go on to enter a trade at the age of 15.

Once in high school, however, I was soon inducted into the school choir, where I learned to read plainsong, which is built on modal scales, and sang as lead treble (boy soprano) until my voice broke. When that happened, my music teacher, a delightful man called Jim Morrison, picked up on it immediately and told me to bring a book with me in future. He didn't care what kind of book, he just didn't want me singing after that. For a whole year, he didn't let me sing a note, and then I went straight to lead baritone, which I sang until I finished school. I sang in the male voice choir in college, too. So although I am musically illiterate, I have had years of experience singing in choirs and ensembles, and I have a quick ear for both melody and harmony and an almost infallible ear for lyrical rhythm and musical tempo. If a song strikes me immediately as being wonderful, I can learn it within minutes—the lyrics and melody practically burn themselves into my mind. On the other hand, if a song does *not* appeal to me immediately, I will never learn it completely. I'll learn to play and sing it, but if I don't keep singing it I'll forget it very quickly.

In July 1968, I performed my first professional gig, in the grandstand show of the Calgary Stampede. That year the Stampede theme was "Salute to the Immigrants," and the first-string headliners, as they were called, included Frank Sinatra Jr. and Tennessee Ernie Ford, while the star of the whole thing, the parade marshal, was an actor named Peter Breck, one of the most recognizable faces in North America that year because of his role as Nick Barkley on television's *The Big Valley*, starring Barbara Stanwyck. I was one of the second-string headliners, and proud to be so. I sang the opening number, a medley of stirring, up-tempo Scots songs, accompanied by the Grandstand Show Pit Orchestra, a full band of Highland pipes and drums, a 23-voice choir and the touring kick line of the Radio City Rockettes. It was quite a debut.

On opening night, I was approached by a bona fide theatrical agent who smooth-talked me into signing an exclusive service contract with his agency, Rojak Artists of Edmonton. Neither he nor I knew it at the time, but that was the first step toward my making a name for myself, many years later, as the only Scots entertainer to be found singing Jewish, French and Afrikaans songs in a Chinese restaurant in southern Alberta. True, so help me. It was at the Oriental Gardens restaurant on Macleod Trail in Calgary, and I sang there, off and on, from about 1977 to 1984.

But there I was in 1968, a headliner in the show I had dreamed for years of seeing, and instead of sitting in the bleachers watching the parade go by I was being driven in my own car in the parade—a 1932 Ford convertible with my name on the sides—with Aunt Janetta up in the bleachers, watching me go by. And throughout the entire event, the matter of job security never entered my mind.

I had made the leap and taken the risk, and had signed a contract with an agent. I knew already that I could support my family by my own efforts, doing the thing I loved to do most at that time. What I did not know was that my marriage, well on the rocks by then, would fall apart completely within the next 15 months, ending in an acrimonious divorce that would deprive me of my son and daughter for many years.

Be that as it may, however, the leap into "show biz" taught me one of the most valuable lessons life has to offer: security lives inside you, if it lives at all, and you take it with you everywhere you go and every time you move. Since then I have never hesitated before changing boats, or even horses, in midstream, provided the upcoming challenge will lead to things I have never experienced before.

And so it was that I eventually moved south, in the dead of winter in 1969, for a five-week engagement as a lounge singer/entertainer at the Tradewinds Hotel in Calgary, which was one of the city's bastions of entertainment at that time. And that's where I started writing again, albeit very tentatively and with no desire to write the great Canadian epic. I had simply arrived at a point in my life when the creative juices started bubbling again. I started looking around me more curiously, observing more keenly, and suddenly found myself almost driven to record what I was seeing and describe what was going on around me.

Being an entertainer in western Canada was about being up on your hockey and football stats and knowing when to sit down, put away the guitar and shut up. It was also about country music. And so I learned a lot of country songs and wrote more than a few, too, some of them more successful than others. "Hurtin' songs" were always the most popular, next to "Somebody-done-somebody-wrong songs." I was in the mood for both kinds back then, and so I wrote some.

Saturday Night Lounge

Hockey Night in Canada,
Nearing overtime,
Every eye is on the screen;
Singing is a crime.

Put that guitar down, boy,
Have yourself a scotch,
Get down and join the playoff crowd,
Come on, sit down and watch.

Montreal Canadiens really playing strong,
Gonna whip these Flyers—this thing won't take long.
Three games out of seven, this'll be the fourth,
And Canada's old Stanley Cup
Will come right back up north.

The Ghost of Your Love

By just turning my head I can see you
Sitting there at the edge of my sight;
Six months after you walked out on me you
Come back here to haunt me tonight.
Every evening I stand here and sing songs,

An' the folks know I'm singing 'bout you;
'Though they don't know your name they accord you the fame
Of the Lady who's keeping me blue,
For the ghost of your love keeps me cryin'

In the night when the lights have gone out,
An' I can't stop my memory from sighin'
A' the trying is wearing me out.
I've been waiting for this night to happen

Every night since my heartbreak began;
Waiting for that main door to swing open
And for you to walk in with a man.
And tonight's the night, baby, you did it!

You just proved I've been living a lie.
You took all the love we had and hid it
In a deep hole to wither and die.

Yet the ghost of that love keeps me cryin'

In the night when the lights are all out,
And I can't stop my memory from sighin'
And the trying is wearing me out.

But, just turning my head, I can see you
Sitting there at the edge of my sight
And a small voice is saying to me you
Let me off the wagon tonight,

So I'm turnin' an' smiling right at you
And the hurt isn't hurting no more,
An' I'm feel in' good now, knowin' that you'll
Never hurt me again like before,

For the ghost of your love's laid to rest now;
There'll be no more crying for me!
I can live, and give living my best now,
For I know now, at last, that I'm free.

  Looking back on that period, it seems to me now that I always carried a notebook and pens with me, and I never had a moment's trouble deciding what to write about next, because there was always something new demanding my attention. I felt like a man who had been starved for years and suddenly found himself in a land flowing with milk and honey. I threw myself into an orgy of writing, and when all else failed, there was the Calgary weather, always ready to be different next time you turned around and to make new demands on your descriptive faculties.

Calgary Winter's Day, 1978

Passing cars—
Just shapeless blobs of colour passing by,
Moving blobs of motion that impinge upon the eye
Without demanding anything
Or needing a reply in terms of focus:
Greyness blotched with melting snow

And stark unfriendly trees
And people crossing, hurried, huddled,
Hunched against the breeze
That cuts through all their clothing
And ignores their silent pleas
For warmth and kindness.
Suddenly, two laughing faces with a magic
Of their own that lets them ignore traffic
And sad trees that stand alone
In their weltering cold slush-piles
While the wind cuts to the bone of all around them
Giggle happily in passing by my window
And are gone, regardless,
And a big blue bus coughs loudly
As it staggers on its way
And a gravel truck behind it waits for it
To clear the way
And the only sound of happiness that's
Passed this way today
Is quickly smothered in the drabness
Of this ghastly winter's day.

Those five weeks at the Tradewinds flew by, and while there I was offered other gigs in the city. My involvement with Calgary—my new life, as it turned out to be—had begun. Within 18 months I had moved there permanently, and, with the exception of the odd out-of-town engagement in places like Red Deer and Edmonton, where I sang mostly at the Chateau Lacombe and Edmonton Inn, and in Lethbridge, where I performed frequently at the Royal Canadian Legion, I stayed in Calgary and thrived and wrote like a demented soul for the next 18 years.

Calgary, without dispute, was the second-best thing that ever happened to me. I can't say it was the best because of a lady I met in Red Deer, Alberta. Her name is Beverley, and she is, beyond doubt or argument, the absolute best thing that has ever happened to me. Every book I have written is dedicated to her, for without her encouragement and patience over the past 30-odd years, they would never have been written, and I would not be the person I am today. Putting up with my shenanigans and idiosyncrasies and providing me with a stable environment in which I could stretch and grow, Beverley made it possible for me to write—the only thing I have ever really wanted to do.

Buy, Sell and Trade

I once met a man—can't remember his name—
Who insisted that trade was a sure way to fame.
He said, "Buster, I'll tell you, ain't nothing that's made
That a smart operator can't buy, sell or trade.
I was strolling along on a quiet little street
Kinda humming a song, never dreaming I'd meet
With the girl who would lead me along by the nose
For the rest of my life, as the old story goes.
It was warm for November, as I can recall,
Old man Time had forgotten to call off the Fall,
But I'll never remember the impulse that made
Me stop by that old store where they buy, sell and trade.
In old Calgary town where the warm Chinook blows,
I was caught off my guard by a sweet prairie rose
And no words could mean more than the vows that we made
By the furniture store where they buy, sell and trade.
I just glanced through the window, not looking no place,
And her smile shook me up like a slap in the face,
And though hindsight is easy, it still kinda seems
That her face all my life had been haunting my dreams.
In the space of that smile my decision was made,
Surely I could find something to buy, sell or trade?
I stepped off of the sidewalk and into the store
And my poor, selfish heart wasn't mine anymore.
Now long years have gone by and the city has grown
And my true love, she died and left me all alone,

But our love sure made nonsense of what that guy said,
For her memory's one thing he can't buy, sell or trade.

What I said there, providing me with a stable environment, sounds simple enough, but in reality, the adjustments Beverley was willing to make are awe inspiring. When I arrived in Calgary, I was what folks in the UK would call "an itinerant musician of no fixed abode." Recently divorced, I literally lived in whatever hotel was employing me—accommodation was written into my musicians'-union contracts. So when Beverley opted to share my life, this was the situation she accepted.

I know she thought it would be fun to live in hotels—and it was, for about a week. Of course, there *are* distinct advantages to hotel living: no dishwashing, no housework. Someone comes in every day and remakes the beds, changes the linen and vacuums the floor. And then there's the cachet of eating out every day rather than having to cook . . . Well, some of the first truths a hard-core restaurant patron learns are that a hamburger is a hamburger is a hamburger, from coast to coast to coast; that a food's description on the menu is usually far better and more stimulating than the food itself; and that the true symbol of Canada should be the zucchini rather than the maple leaf, for while the maple is largely indigenous only to central Canada, the zucchini is found in eateries of all kinds from St. John's, Newfoundland, to Victoria, BC, to Churchill, Manitoba. After an astonishingly short time of eating in restaurants and cafés, you reach the stage at which you would happily kill for a simple home-cooked meal.

Beverley and I lasted about a year as hotel dwellers—an inordinately *long* year—before we accepted the fact that we were likely going to stay in Calgary indefinitely, at which point we started casting about for a real place to live. The first apartment we rented was a furnished upper floor of an old house in Inglewood, which cost $75 a month, utilities included. We loved it there, and there, for really the first time ever, I settled down with a typewriter as a constant companion and physical presence in my life. It's hard now to imagine using a typewriter, accustomed as we are to being able to insert, revise, cut and paste electronically; I wonder how I and other writers back then ever managed to get anything down.

To My Typewriter

Hello, machine, long time no see!
Do I seem strange as you to me?
I know you're mine to have and love
When inspirations push and shove
Their noisy and ebullient ways
Into the time frames of my days;
I know that strangeness should not be
Applicable to you and me;
I know that we are man and wife,
Master and mistress, fork and knife,
Civet and vixen, bat and ball,
Melded together over all.
But I've been playing shy of late,
Ignoring you, making you wait,
Walking away for other things;
Waiting for what the future brings;
Dodging the present, lying low;
Being irresponsible, I know!
Being afraid's more like the truth . . .
I've chickened out, to speak thee sooth . . .
I'm scared, somehow, to try to write
What's in my head; I guess I might
Be justifiably afraid
That dust and rust and lust have made
My functions falter and decay
To this point where they stand today . . .

THE ENTERTAINER

But how ridiculously quaint
That I should come to what I ain't:
A moral coward, shorn, and blue,
And scared, dear IBM, of you!

My arrival in Calgary in the spring of 1969, the year following my first visit to the Calgary Stampede, was the start of the most electrifying awakening I had ever experienced. I can recall being unimpressed at first, because the highest building in the downtown area, other than the spectacular and then-newly completed Husky Tower by the Canadian Pacific Railway station, was the circular tower of the Summit Hotel, which housed the city's most highly hyped nightclub on its 10th floor. At first glance I saw nothing lovely at all, certainly nothing to compare with Edmonton's graceful Alberta Government Telephones building, which struck me when I first saw it as one of the most beautiful and functional high-rise buildings I had ever seen. Strange as that may be, I still feel the same way about the old AGT building 40 years later, and I don't think I have ever been inside it. Nostalgia, I suppose.

The population of Calgary then, in 1969, was somewhere around 280,000. When I left in 1986, it had grown to 560,000, and by 2007 it was over a million. Huge growth brings huge changes, and when I go back there now I don't recognize much beyond the downtown core. The suburbs have become another place altogether. I recall what some wag once said about the city of Glasgow: "It would have been a beautiful place if they'd built it out in the country." But when I first got to Calgary all those years ago, what astounded me was that this city, vibrant, humming and full of life, was not yet 100 years old. As a European immigrant, I found this newness simply stunning, verging upon the incomprehensible, and a few years later I wrote"Cherchez La Femme."

60

JACK WHYTE: FORTY YEARS IN CANADA

Cherchez La Femme

There's the juiciest scandal that I can recall
Going on now, world wide, it appears.
There's a female, of course, at the root of it all.
Spreading joy, anger, laughter and tears.
She's a lady, some say; others call her a whore;
But though everyone knows who she is,
What she is, what her motives are, no one is sure,
And no one man can claim her as His!

A true daughter of Eve, she is wild, unrestrained
In her passionate loving of life.
And each one of her lovers—man's folly's ingrained—
Seeks to break her and take her to wife.
She's exquisitely lovely; an emperor's bride
With a shape that's the pure stuff of dreams
And the rich joie de vivre that bubbles inside
Her could light up the whole world, it seems.

All the media adore her. She steals every show
And her face adorns news stands, world-wide;
She is pictured in all weathers, sun, rain and snow;
She's the essence of beauty and pride.
So her face and her costumes, her wealth and her looks
Are exploited for all that they're worth.
She's the ultimate symbol; the subject of books;
She's the richest heiress on this earth.

Though men lust for her body and covet her youth
With a hunger that's huge and obscene,
She remains, somehow, virtuous, armoured in truth
With an innocence vast and serene,
And she shines with a glory that's huge and extreme
With a lustre that's richer than gold:
She's Alberta, triumphant; Alberta, supreme,
And she's seventy-five years old!

Calgary, I discovered, was a highly charged place that some people called cattle country and others called the oil patch, where mounted cowboys had been known to ride right into the lobby of the Palliser Hotel during the week-long Calgary Stampede; where the high-flying movers and shakers of the oil industry met daily to conduct multimillion-dollar business in the sanctuary of the Petroleum Club—the Pete, to its habitués—and the cattle breeders and ranchers met at the staid but luxurious Ranchmen's Club. It was, in short—and it took me a long time to figure this out and to identify what it was about the city that so enthralled me—a place, an entire domain, of hope and faith the likes of which I had never before encountered.

In Calgary, I discovered, there were no limitations on what a man could do, other than the limitations he imposed upon himself. There were none of the restrictive rules and frowning, disapproving governing criteria that I had found everywhere else: no generically entrenched class system into which one was born with no hope of ever escaping, and no inbuilt system of exclusion. Certainly there was a hierarchy of power, but it was based on success, hard work, business ethics and acumen, not on birth, innate privilege and the proper old-school tie. You might have come from the most obscure background and own nothing today, but, by God, if you wanted to put in the time and effort and eventually strike it rich in whatever you did, even to a modest degree, then no one was going to stand in the way of your joining whatever clubs and organizations you want to join.

I didn't really see that at first, and could not have appreciated it even if I had: I had spent my entire life to that point, 29 years, accepting censure and disapproval at every turn, because I had been taught to do that since I was a child. Only slowly did I come to see that my staple diet since infancy had been frowning disapproval of everything I loved and enjoyed, and third-party anticipation of my failing at everything I tried to do. Now here was a place where nobody cared what I did and no one had preconceived notions of what I would do, could do or ought to do, and a place, too, where I would be accepted and applauded if I worked hard and excelled at whatever I did decide to do. This was Calgary in the early 1970s, and it set me free in a way I had never known before. It set me free to look back on the teaching career I had enjoyed so much at first, and to look forward to my new life as an entertainer, responsible for my own success through the exercising of my own talents and abilities.

And then I realized, to my great amusement, that being an entertainer was not so different from being a teacher. In the classroom I had sat in isolation on a raised platform in the corner of a large room filled with disinterested and mildly bored people who had lives of their own to lead and were there, putting up with me, only because they had to be. My task every day was to capture their attention, banish their boredom, engage their curiosity and, I hoped, send them home at the end of each day with a little more knowledge than they had when they came in.

As an entertainer, I sat in isolation every evening on a raised platform in the corner of a large room filled with disinterested and mildly bored people who had lives of their own to lead and were there, putting up with me, only because they had to be there in order to get a drink. My task every night was to capture their attention, banish their boredom, engage their curiosity and, I hoped, send them home at the end of each night with a little more knowledge than they had when they came in. *Plus ça change, plus c'est la même chose* . . .

Whyte as the regimental bard

CHAPTER FOUR

THE BARBAROUS BARD

Since 1977, I have taken great pride in, and derived great pleasure from, being the regimental bard of the Calgary Highlanders, and I have also found much enjoyment in the questions associated with that title. Most people, upon hearing it, blink mildly in perplexity, then think about it for a few moments before biting the bullet and coming straight out with the next question: "What is a bard and what does he do?"

The best answer to that question I ever came up with—and I said it flippantly at the time, only realizing as the words emerged that it was absolutely correct—is that a bard's job is to make people cry. A bard is a tribal poet charged with the responsibility of safeguarding, recording and retelling the tribe's history in a way that is viscerally exciting and memorable, so that it stirs up the emotions of everyone who encounters it. And invariably, since the dawn of history, the most effective method of doing that has been orally, with songs and poems—narrative poems in which the message, the morality and the appeal to tradition and basic emotions are direct, simple, powerful and unmistakable.

That responsibility became mine when I agreed to become the bard of the Calgary Highlanders back in the late '70s. This regiment, raised during the First World War as the 10th Canadian Battalion of Foot, came of age, like all the other Canadian units, with the capture of Vimy Ridge during the Somme offensive in 1916. But its strongest claim to fame during the war, and its most outstanding battle honour, was won several months before the Somme offensive, during the Battle of Ypres, at a place called St. Julien Wood, in April 1915. In recognition of the gallantry of its personnel during that encounter, the battalion was awarded the honour of wearing a stylized oak leaf—a symbol of the oak trees in the wood—in its official cap badge. That may not seem like much of a distinction nowadays, when we have been separated from such things by almost 60 years of more or less unbroken peace, but 90 years ago, during a war that killed millions of soldiers, such symbols had great meaning and deep significance.

When I began my sojourn as regimental bard, few, if any, of the young soldiers and officers of the regiment who attended the formal mess dinners—and they look younger to me with every passing year— had any notion of what their forebears had really done, or what they had achieved when it came time to prove their mettle, and that was something I had to change. Fortunately, the regimental history of the First World War had been written by a gifted writer, and through his eyes I was able to imagine the events that had occurred at St. Julien.

St. Julien Wood, April 1915

Five hundred yards to the front, a black silhouette stood
Outlined by the flickering gunfire; St. Julien Wood.
The land in between had been battered and pillaged and raped
And, concealed by the black, smoking craters, the gates of Hell gaped.
Canadian Soldiers stood, waiting for word to advance,
Their minds drinking in this grim vision of beautiful France
While their ears cringed in mental discomfort and physical pain
At the noise of the barrage that screamed around Ypres again.

The time came, and they moved out, advancing in alternate waves
Each two companies strong; each one moving as water behaves,
Flowing forward in silence, to find its own level around
All the up flung confusion of shell-tortured, treacherous ground.
In spite of the darkness of midnight, the going was good
So that, still undetected, their front ranks came close to the Wood
Until, just as the forest developed a visible edge,
They ran into the French farmer's border—a strong, healthy hedge!
What to do? There was no way around it, and time was their foe
Just as much as the Germans; smash through, there's nowhere else to go.
So they tried, and they died, row on row, as though caught in barbed wire
As the enemy, startled alert, laid down murderous fire.
Decimated—each tenth man laid dead—was a word coined in Rome,
And the Tenth would have happily settled for that, and gone home,
But the hedge all around them confined them, and try as they would,
They had no way but forward to go . . . To St. Julien Wood.
They were out of the hedge now, and into the enemy trench
Swinging bayonet and rifle butt, covered in mud, blood and stench,
And then out of the trench and on, up to the edge of trees
Where the enemy, hidden by tree trunks, could snipe them with ease.
But the surging Canucks were demented by now—men possessed
By one single and burning incentive: to clean out this nest
Of Demonic and venomous hornets; this devil-spawned brood
Who were trying to stop them from taking St. Julien Wood.
And the Hun staggered backward, his dead lying heaped on the ground;
Hundreds tried to surrender, appalled by the fury they'd found
In these madmen who fought like blind Furies unleashed by the gods,
Coming forward, and winning, in spite of incredible odds!
But then, somehow, the stunned German infantry rallied again
And perceived that the demons who tore at them really were men,
And from enfilade points they set up a new, withering fire
That would force these Canadian berserkers to stop and retire.
Those first three hellish hours dragged on to become sixty four;
Almost three solid days of exhaustion, gas, gunfire and gore,
And only one hundred of eight hundred and sixteen men
Came back out of St. Julien Wood into sunlight again.
What they did in that wood, amid carnage and slaughter and strife,

THE BARBAROUS BARD

Moved their General to say that the things he most prized in his life
Were the "Canada" armlet displayed with such pride on his sleeve
And the honour he felt, just to know what his men had achieved.

Refrain:
For as machine guns spewed at them
And shell fire chewed at them
The tired survivors had no water and no food
Because for sixty hours
They'd defied the powers
Of the Kaiser's crack battalions at St. Julien Wood.
The place had been the test of them;
Had seen the best of them
Blown into glory in the battle's bitter feud,
And the oak leaf medallion
Of the Tenth Battalion
Is the symbol of its glory at St. Julien Wood.
Loud sing the bugles that sound in November,
Calling the Living to pause and remember
Arthur; Lowrie; Ormond; Boyle;
Comrades resting after battle's toil . . .
So when the mess kit's sparkling
And the pibroch's darkling
Melody brings goose flesh and a stirring in the blood
You know the rank and file and
Brethren of the Highlanders
Are reliving the glory of St. Julien Wood.

Writing a poem to celebrate the regiment's prowess in the Second
World War, however, was a different kettle of fish, and I became acutely
aware, early on in the research process, of the vast difference between
the official regimental histories of the two world wars. The first was
inspirational, engaging and visceral; the second, by comparison, was
stodgy, prosaic and pedestrian. Reportorial and tediously trite at times,
it made no attempt to offer any kind of insight, even editorial, into the

motivations or purposes of the people involved in the various actions, and those overtones of pomposity and tedium had a depressing effect on my creative juices. I simply could not find a "hook" on which to hang my narrative, despite the fact that the specific action involved—the capture of the heavily defended Walcheren Causeway on the Scheldt Estuary—was an outstanding one with several unique aspects to it, which should have made it easy to write about. Try as I would, however, I couldn't find that hook and nothing was happening in my Creative Department.

I must have started to write a dozen poems, perhaps even more, but none of them went anywhere and eventually I began to experience flutterings of panic as I became increasingly aware of the inexorable approach of the annual Walcheren mess dinner. And as the last week came along, I found myself flinching at the prospect of going empty-handed to the formal dinner at which my new regimental battle poem was to be presented for the first time. I knew the function would draw a profusion of visiting "brass" from all over Canada and probably some high-ranking military visitors from the US, for this was the second-most-important event of the regimental year, after the St. Julien Dinner in April. And then, at the very last minute—it was actually two nights before the event—I had a sudden breakthrough and everything fell into place. I must have known the crucial piece of information that contained my "hook" all along, but for some ineluctable reason the significance of the datum had escaped me for months: the battle of the Walcheren Causeway had taken place on October 31, 1944—Halloween!

The Walcheren Causeway, October 31, 1944

I recall I sat on the porch that night,
Sipping whisky, straight and neat,
Watching tiny goblins and lanterns bright

Flitting up and down the street,
But I don't recall his approach at all;
He just suddenly came into view
Standing straight and tall by the garden wall,
And I greeted him as I would you:
"Good evening, soldier. God save the Queen.
Sit down, man, and slake your thirst
With some good malt Scotch, for it's Halloween,
October the thirty-first.

The kids are all out in the neighbourhood
And I'm drinking some quiet toasts
To the wee folk, there, to my own childhood,
To the darkness and the ghosts ..."
He turned and eyed me; I'd never seen
His face in my life before.
"Sure," he said, "I'll be happy to toast Halloween—
Halloween, nineteen-forty-four."
He crossed the lawn and he shook my hand
And I cheerfully poured him a glass.
I assumed, from his clothing, he played in a band—
He was kilted, and glittering with brass.
He proposed, "The Calgary Highlanders!"
We downed it. I poured us one more.
"To the Walcheren Causeway," he said, "Halloween,
Nineteen hundred and forty four!"
"To the what?" I asked, and his eyes went blank
And a strange look came over his face
And, embarrassed, I flushed, and my spirits sank,
For I felt myself, somehow, disgraced.
"The Walcheren Causeway." He said it again.
"It's a roadway; a long, narrow belt
Of a road, built out over the water and fen
To a Dutch island, out on the Scheldt.
Just a high, built-up roadway; flat, narrow, exposed
To the wind and the rain and the sleet.
God! The first time we saw it, we never supposed
We'd be crossing the thing on our feet!

"It was two thousand yards long, and each narrow foot
Of it made it a breeze to defend
For the Germans who held it. You see, they could shoot
From the roadblock they'd built at their end.
I know two thousand yards might not seem a long way
When you're taking a stroll with your sons,
But at night, in a fight, it's a bloody long way
Looking right down an enemy's guns.
"They had told us, at first, we'd be crossing in boats
To assault Middelburg 'cross the Slooe,
But the mud was as thick as the fear in our throats
And it stuck our assault craft like glue.
But we had to cross over, we had to attack,
And by land, there was only one route
And that route was the Causeway, straight, long, bare and black.
Well, the Highlanders moved in on foot,
Under cover of darkness, with no place to halt,
No surprise, no manoeuvring room;
Just a mad, midnight dash—a straight frontal assault
Into madness, confusion, and doom.
Gerry's mortars and field guns were well zeroed in,
And the roadblock machine guns as well,
But we had to approach them, engage them, and win,
So we charged them like bats out of hell!
"All the guns, theirs and ours, turned the night into day
And the shell splinters, bullets and stone
Fragments turned the air solid, and slaughtered men lay
Where they fell, lifeless, limp and alone.
Twelve Platoon of B Company took the full force
Of the hellish, defensive cross fire;
They were out in the front, unprotected, of course,
And, too soon, they were forced to retire.
"Daylight came, and the sight of that shell-splintered road
Would have riven an Archangel's brain,
But D Company moved forward and took up the load
And the whole place erupted again.
How they did it, God knows, but they went all the way

To where no sane man could hope to survive,
And they captured the pillbox, they carried the day,
And the rest of us walked in alive.
"Like the Light Brigade charging the jaws of death,
Riding into the mouth of Hell,
They smelled the stink of the Demon's breath
As their friends and their messmates fell.
Like their Highlander forebears who fought with pride
On the rolling Zulu veldt,
They faced extinction and stemmed its tide
On that Causeway over the Scheldt.
"Like their Sister Regiment's Thin Red Line
On the Balaclava clay,
They defied false gods for the narrow spine
Of the Walcheren Causeway.
As the Calgary men took Saint Julien
In the War that had gone before,
These ones captured the Causeway to Walcheren
And distinguished the oak leaf they wore."
His voice tailed away, and he stared at me,
And between us a silence hung;
As I reached for the bottle to charge his glass,
I was thinking he looked too young
To have seen the things he said he'd seen,
But then shock unhinged my jaw,
For the chair sat empty where he had been
And the night had turned cold and raw.
I jumped up and ran to the garden wall
And I searched the empty street,
But I saw no sign of him at all,
I heard no sound of feet.
Then his voice said, clearly, "To Walcheren,
Don't forget!" inside my head,
And I shivered and turned, and went slowly in
To a sleepless, comfortless bed.

One guest at the regimental dinner that Walcheren night made it his business to enlist me to write a piece for his organization. His name was Hugh MacMillan, and he was a prominent Calgary architect, but he was also a member of a quasi-military group that was a reincarnation of the old 78th Fraser Highlanders of Canada, which had been raised by Lord Simon Fraser and had stormed the Plains of Abraham with General Wolfe. The Frasers' recently established regimental HQ was in Quebec City, where they had established a drum and musket corps for cadets, equipping them with copies of the original uniforms worn by Fraser's clansmen and, of course, drums and muskets. MacMillan wanted me to write a poem for the Frasers, doing for them and for the Plains of Abraham what I had done for the Calgary Highlanders and St. Julien and Walcheren.

I went away and thought about it for a while, did some reading and research and then wrote "Abraham's Eve," which I have always liked because of the way it falls into two sections, the first furtive and tense during the approach and the scaling of the cliffs to Quebec, and the second martial and staccato, rendering the rhythm and tempo of the regimental drums summoning the troops to action.

Abraham's Eve

In the darkness of midnight the flat bottomed boats
Packed around the fleet's flagship were barely afloat;
They were loaded with soldiers, and loaded they'd stay
Until light from one lantern should send them away.

In the lead boat, two French-speaking Officers stood,
Looking out for their General's welfare and good
As he sat by their side on a hard, wooden bench,
Chewing over his thoughts for subduing the French.

They were Donald MacDonald and young Simon Fraser,
Both Highlander Captains, both destined trail blazers,

For theirs were the talents, the eyes and the feet
That would lead Wolfe to glory or bitter defeat.
Two a.m., and the lantern was hauled to the shrouds.
As the boats began moving, no man spoke aloud.
Their line stretched on water for four hundred yards
And the tide was fast ebbing; the rowing was hard.

As the lead boat approached land, a shout came: "qui vive?"
Captain Fraser called, quietly, "France! France, et vive
Le Roi," praying his accent would pass him as French
While his guts turned to water and fear made him blench.

Yet another called out: "A quel regiment? Hein?"
Fraser, swallowing, answered, "The Queen's! De la Reine!"
But the sentry complained that the words were not clear.
"Shut your mouth, fool!" hissed Fraser, "The English might hear!"

"Let them pass," cried another voice, further along,
"They're just bringing our rations. What took them so long?"
Fraser waited for more, his heart loud in his chest,
But the guards were now quiet; the lead boat pulled west.

Two hours later, still silent, men clambered ashore
Stretching limbs that were cramped; straight'ning backs that were sore,
And looked upwards in darkness, each craning his neck
At the cliffs that towered up there, protecting Quebec.

(Drum Tempo)

It was Fraser and MacDonald who were first to climb the slope,
Captains of the Fighting Frasers, in the dark they had to grope,
And in stumbling up the steep path, through a swift and rocky stream,
They surprised a watchful picket who gave challenge with a scream!

But MacDonald answered quickly, they'd been sent down from Quebec
To relieve the lonely outpost and conduct surveillance checks
On the sentries at their posts, to see that vigilance was high,
And it almost seemed to work, until the sentry raised the cry!

Then the hunt was up! but those poor, sleepy French Militiamen
Were too startled to be quick, so they were put to sleep again!

In ten minutes from the landing, to the taking of the post,
Every living Frenchman on that path had given up the ghost!

The remainder of the night was spent in climbing up the rock:
Forty seven hundred men had gained the Heights by six o'clock,
With eleven hundred Frasers flashing tartan in the dawn
And full eighteen hundred muskets when the battle lines were drawn.

They were grand, the Fighting Frasers, on the Plains of Abraham
When James Wolfe and Simon Fraser brought destruction to Montcalm,
Though today the Plains of Abraham, so gentle, so at peace,
Give no hint about the fury that destroyed the Fleur de Lys.

But in fifteen bloody, brutal minutes there, below Quebec,
France's Colony in Canada went down, a total wreck:
Fifteen godless, mindless minutes, and the Plains of Abraham
Drank the blood of martial princes: English Wolfe, and French Montcalm.

In 1974, for reasons I'll discuss elsewhere in this book, I wrote, directed and appeared in a one-man show on the life of Robert Burns, the iconic Scottish poet whose genius is celebrated worldwide every year on or close to his birthday, January 25, wherever Scots and wannabe Scots can gather. Very few non-Scots nowadays even know who he was, but he is, in fact, the second-most-quoted source in the English language after the King James Bible, ahead of both Shakespeare in third place and Karl Marx in fourth. .

Burns has always fascinated me, and when I was young and intolerant it used to outrage me that people should be wilfully unaware of his greatness. I called my show *Rantin', Rovin' Robin—A Night With Robert Burns* and crossed Canada with it several times, eventually performing it in almost every theatre in the country. My musical director–accompanist was a wonderful musician called Jo Hansen, and he and I saw a lot of this country together.

My main motivation in writing the piece was to make Burns, the man and his works—he had been dead for more than 200 years by then—more intelligible, transparent and human to non-Scots Canadians. I was on stage as Burns for two solid hours, with a 15-minute intermission, and in that time I led my audiences through the high and low points of his life, sang 15 of his best-known songs and recited all of his greatest poems, some of them in their entirety and others in abridged versions. During this time I acquired a reputation for being an "expert" on Burns, a reputation that led, inevitably, to a proliferation of invitations from various clubs and societies to attend their annual Burns celebrations. In consequence, for more years than I care to recollect now, during the last week and a half of January and the first week and a half of February, I travelled the length and breadth of Canada and the US, performing and officiating at Robbie Burns suppers, dinners and celebrations, so much so that Beverley used to say I would end up, every February, suffering from third-degree Burns.

That same reputation led to my being invited in 1976 to join the half-dozen Calgary fellows who were considering starting up a Burns Club in Calgary. They were, in alphabetical order, Don Cameron, Alastair Ross, Alistair Sinclair, Graham Underwood, Bob Watson and John Whitelock. I became the seventh, and I was the bard right from the outset. There had been previous incarnations of the Burns Club in Calgary, but they had all died out naturally as the members grew older and failed to recruit new blood. We decided that we would do things differently, and we started by restricting the number of full club members to 37—one member for each year of the poet's life. That way, we hoped, we might eventually make full membership something to be aspired to. And it worked. Today there are still only 37 full, voting members, but there is a large group of associate and social members, and the waiting list for full membership is impressive.

In the first year, we held meetings in our own homes, but by the second year we had more than doubled our membership, and it became a priority to find appropriate premises in which to meet. Fortunately, I had met that same year an amiable and admirable man called George Rose, who owned and operated one of the first and most successful high-end townhouse rental developments in Calgary. It was known as Brae Glen, and it had a wonderful, superbly equipped clubhouse, complete with auditorium and wet-bar lounge, called the Brae Glen Club. We thought that it would be a natural home for the Calgary Burns Club.

George was a congenial fellow, and very proud of his Scots heritage. He and I had come to know each other through the Calgary Highlanders, and as I had recently moved into one of his rental units I was charged with the task of "selling" the idea to him. It didn't take much. The poem that follows, written in the verse form known as "the Burns stanza," did the trick in record time. For those of my readers unfamiliar with the Scots language and idiom, I can promise that close scrutiny of the words (and the bracketed hints) will make the outlandish dialect marginally more comprehensible.

A letter to George Rose, of Brae Glen, Braeside Drive, Calgary, soliciting the use of his beautiful premises at the Brae Glen Club for the monthly meetings of the Burns Club

Nae doubt ye must be wondering who
Would write like this, in verse, to you . . .
In proper, Burnsian stanzas, too,
And for what reason?
I hope that when you've read this through,
Ye'll find it pleasin'.

My fellow members thought it might
Be fun for their Bard, one Jack Whyte,

To strain and strive wi' words, to fight,
Time and again,
To write a Burnsian letter, bright
And brief, ye ken?

We have a problem, Mr. Rose,
Thornier than one might suppose—
One, I must add, who little knows
Of Clubs and meetings,
For as a healthy, fine Club grows,
There's aye the seating!

For though eight members may foregather
In ae small room an' crack thegether [*talk among themselves*]
Wi' ne'er a thought o' wind or weather,
Eight's still a wheen [*a bunch*]!
But a sma' room shrinks like a burnt feather
When there's sixteen!

We havena' got the room now, George,
To meet in comfort for to forge
Our Club's way forward—we'd engorge
A living room,
And halls for rent are a' too large
And cauld's the tomb [*cold as a tomb*]!

So we wad like to make Brae Glen
Our Club's official hame, ye ken?
There's muckle room for eighteen men [*lots of room*]
To meet at ease
On Sunday mornings, now and then,
Tae shoot the breeze.

Our Business Meetings hence will be
Confined to one month out o' three;
One Sunday, when the room is free.
We'll keep it clean,
And when we've gaun, nane will e'er see
Whaur we ha'e been.

We'd like to have a copy made
O' our Club Charter, and displayed
Expensively, wi' Class, (gowd braid!) [*gold braid*]
Upo' your wa'. [*Upon your wall*]
We're proud o' it, when all is said,
Baith great and sma'.

Our Club memorabilia
Would soon become familiar,
'Though we'd no gild the lily, or
Abuse your trust
By showing aething silly or
Just gathering dust.

This then, George, is our Club's request:
We think your Lounge would suit us best;
It's airy, clean an' nicely dressed,
A fitting hame
For Calgary's Burns Club to attest
To the Bard's name

So, if ye would, please, gi'e some thought
As to whether we may, or not,
Make use o' that delightful spot
And call it hame.
We'd bring renown, as like as not,
To Brae Glen's name!

So now I'll thank ye in advance.
I hope that you'll no' look askance
On this request, nor let your glance
Frown to a glower?
Call me, or Graham, and give's the chance
To talk it ower.

And if the problem's one o' rent,
I think the coin might worse be spent.
Though guid Scots broadcloth might be rent [*torn*]
Wi' thrift-born grief,
The thought o' meetings in a tent

THE BARBAROUS BARD

Defies belief!

I'm finished now, I've had my say.
I'll send this and await the day
I hear from you; meantime, I'll pray
You'll see the proof
The Calgary Burns Club should stay
'Neath Brae Glen's roof.

George was an excellent host, and when the Clydesdale Bank of Scotland issued a five-pound note several years later bearing Burns' likeness, we quickly acquired a brand-new, unblemished one and had it framed and mounted as our token rent, with the following attached:

Dedication to George Rose, of Brae Glen: incorporated into the presentation of the Annual Rental of the Brae Glen Club on November 16, 1978. Rental was a five-pound note, issued by the Clydesdale Bank of Scotland and featuring an engraving of the poet Robert Burns, ploughing (tilling) a field. The banknote was mounted on a parchment scroll, decorated by Bob Sharp and featuring this poem.

Ca' canny, George, and ha'e a drink.
Sit down and loose your collar!
Here's five poun' Scotch, as rent! We think
It's stronger than your Dollar!

We ken it's late – lang owerdue –
And tho' we meant to start wi' it
Lang syne [*long ago*] . . . It's such a bonny blue ,
We couldna bear to part wi'it!

It's legal tender, oil-rich ink,
And solid, lasting siller [*money*];
The Clydesdale Bank will never sink
Wi' Rob Burns at the tiller!

Ten years later, after moving to Vancouver in 1986, I founded another Burns club, and my fondest memories of the Vancouver Burns Club revolve around one of my oldest and dearest friends, Robert Stuart Smith, who sang and entertained professionally for years under the name Robert Stuart. Rob is a brilliantly gifted performer and raconteur whose predilection for the tantalizing toddy led him to climb firmly up onto the wagon more than a decade ago, but before he did, he had a few blessedly bibulous moments that I was happy and delighted to share with him. One of those is the episode of the Athol brose.

Few people outside the Scots community have even heard of Athol brose, and few are the Scots who have drunk it, for Scots in general tend to be a wee bit straitlaced in their conduct and profligate in their disapproval and condemnation of strong drink . . . generally (and wrongly) deemed to have caused the downfall of the ploughman bard himself. Athol brose is lethally strong drink parading under the guise of wondrous delicacy. It is a distillation of oatmeal, heather honey and whisky, and it slips down smoothly and viscously, without the slightest violation to the sensibilities of even wee Scots wifies. The poem "Rob Stuart and the Athol Brose" is modelled upon the work of Robert W. Service, and it deals with one of Rob's more memorable performances, which, unfortunately, I was not around to witness. It was Ladies' Night, when the club members brought their spouses on their annual outing, and it was one of the few such evenings that I had to miss because of a prior long-standing commitment. But I heard about it . . .

Rob Stuart and the Athol Brose

When a Scotsman turns toward Robert Burns
He's inclined to begin to think;
And most Scots in their prime, from time to time,
Have been known to imbibe strong drink,

But you can't do both, though we're seldom loath
To try, and the whole Club knows
Of the Ladies' Night when Rob Stuart got tight
As a tick on Athol Brose.

In the days ahead, it would go unsaid
That poor Rob was not alone;
His was far from being the only star
That night that got overblown,
For when Leckie's hoard was uncapped and poured
And then sniffed, and then sipped, then drunk,
It seems there were few of the Burns Club crew
Who did not get squiffed as skunks!

Yet, the fact remains, like old, long-set stains
In the weft of a worn-out kilt,
That poor Rob can't quite bring to mind that night,
Or the way that his mind went "Tilt!"
He was dead on his feet—he'd had nothing to eat
And he'd been on the run all day—
And the power, he knows, of the Athol Brose
Simply washed his sense away.

He recalls being aware that I couldn't be there
That night, I was booked elsewhere;
So the slim entertainment was all left to him
And the single piano player;
And he freely admits he'd have called it quits
And abandoned the microphone
If the Brose in his snoot, and the wine, to boot
Hadn't flushed him clean to the bone.

So I've noticed him wince, now and then, ever since
He recovered the following day;
He's appalled to recall the occasion at all,
And he's wondering, "What did I say?"
Yet the Ladies all seemed—was that real, or just dreamed?—
Quite amused, and Rob hopes that they were . . .
I know just how he feels, and my knowledge is real

Because, God knows, I've been there!

When you're one of the few who can stand up and do
Things alone, on your own, unafraid,
You respond to the call, when you're called on at all,
And step forward, on parade.
You stand up and perform; but your conduct, your form,
Your behaviour, your language, your skills,
Are all judged and critiqued; and the crowd can be piqued
If you can't cure all their ills.

If you make a wrong move, they disapprove.
If you're drunk, god forbid! heads will shake.
They forget, one and all, they can't stand up at all,
And perform, even sober—they'd break!
And they'll take, on occasion, a lot of persuasion
To see, and accept, and allow
That we'd all live in terror, were every small error
We made burned into our brow!

No man, I think, improves with drink,
That's as true as a wheel has a hub,
But it's been little kenn't in the hours that we've spent
Since we formed our own Burns Club.
"No man is an Island," one poet said,
Burns would say, "We're brothers one and all, man!"
And "'Tis danger to gaze on the wine when 'tis red"
Means "When tight, ye might tip ower and fall, man."

So the play was played and the memories fade
And if Rob's dire sin was the worst
That this Club ever knows as it expands and grows
We may think ourselves lightly cursed . . .
But I watch his eyes, and I sympathize,
And our President does, too,
Because he, like me, before all B.C.
Has performed in a pickled stew . . .

And so here's to Stuart; he's named and empower'd

THE BARBAROUS BARD

Like the Bard we celebrate;
For Robert Burns did a few star turns
Himself, and they call him great.
And here's to our wives; we share their lives,
But we meet in friendship, too!
In Time's feathery mist, we'll all get pissed
Now and then. Most Scotsmen do!

Still, my first and enduring love, in terms of Robbie Burns, was always and ever the Calgary Burns Club, now generally recognized as one of the most enduring and successful in the world, and when I was invited in 1996 to speak at the annual Supper of the Burns Society in St. John's, Newfoundland, I thought it appropriate to adapt a poem I had already written for the Calgary Burns Club, in which I talked about the strange and internationally celebrated Scots phenomenon Robbie Burns.

Some Thoughts On Burns

Januar', when every Scotsman turns
To thoughts, of some kind, on Rob Burns;
While outside, Winter girns [*grimaces*] and squeals
And blows cold snow in whirling reels
To choke the roads and bring despair
To poor folk travelling anywhere . . .

Januar', when all the Old Year's flown
And the brand new one's still unknown,
Its mysteries still fresh and brent [*bright*],
Its messages all still unsent,
Its summer, like a lass's smile
Promising, "Aye, but bide a while . . ."

Januar', when here in St. John's town
For years, now, word has gone aroun'

The Clans are once more gatherin'
For gibberish and blatherin';
To spend a night in pleasure's ring
In praise of Scotland's uncrowned King.

But yet, there's folk in every town
Who have no idea what goes down
When Scotch folk gather here each year
To eat and drink and share good cheer.
They canna see much good ava' [at all]
In haggis, neeps and usquebaugh [turnips and whisky]!

Two hundred years elapsed last year
Since Burns' voice was last heard here
On this good earth, and yet his views
Are still mint-fresh; they're still good news;
Unchanged since Robert first began
To preach the brotherhood of man.

For years I walked, as Burns, on stage;
I held his opinions, felt his rage,
And strove to outline his beliefs,
Extol his joys, explain his griefs
And bring the man to life for those
Who, not being Scots, could ill-suppose

The impact that this peasant chiel [child]
Had on a world so stark, so real,
So grim, so bleak, so thrawn, so dour [so stern, so harsh]
It held one prayer: "God help the Poor!"
A world so drear, our minds today
Just canna grasp the fell, dark sway [awesome, dark power]

That birth and rank had on poor folk
Who, being born, then wore a yoke
Hung on them by "their betters," who
Then ruled their lives and what they'd do.

THE BARBAROUS BARD

Burns, in his time, and with his pen,
Did much to change the world o' men.

With words that rang like striking swords
Deep-dipped in ink, he severed cords
That had held honest men confined
For centuries. So thickly twined
And greasy were these muckle ropes
They slew men's pride and killed their hopes.

Burns changed all that—though not alone—
But through his works, he made it known
To Lord and Lady, wife and bawd,
An honest man's the work o' God
And there's no guarantee on Earth
That good must spring from noble birth.

He it was who, at length, defined
The man of independent mind;
The man who, knowing wheat from chaff,
Can glean the grain and then can laugh
At the stupidity of he
Who's blind to what all others see.

Burns lived and wrote, found time to love,
To recognize the Powers above,
To dream great dreams that men might be
Born free to grow in liberty;
He sowed new thoughts like far flung seeds
And being sown, they grew like weeds.

And so we're here, Burns lovers a'
This night, and Januar' winds may blaw
About the gullied, concrete streets;
But who cares if it snows or sleets?
That's all outside . . . We're here, and glad
To thank God for The Ploughman Lad!

So here's to Newfoundland, and Burns
And many, bright, happy returns
O' this one night in a' the year
When good men meet in honest cheer
To raise a glass in gratitude
To Rob Burns' life and attitude.

THE BARBAROUS BARD

The Ploughman Bard in a Scots baronial mansion (a CBC studio in Vancouver, 1976)

CHAPTER FIVE

THIRD-DEGREE BURNS

So how did I ever become involved with Robert Burns in the first place? Well, I studied him in high school in Scotland, where I learned a number of his most famous poems and sang a dozen or so of his most beautiful songs, but then I forgot about him for a while, until my unfortunate proclivity for never forgetting good lyrics got me into trouble. One of the disadvantages of being a literate Scot entertaining in bars and lounges was that I frequently attracted the late-night attention of bibulously serious fellow Scots who insisted, in their drunken earnestness, upon misquoting and generally mangling Burns' work and reputation, claiming a spiritual brotherhood with the man and yet representing him as an inveterate drunkard and an incorrigible, Rabelaisian whoremonger—a double calumny, rooted in ignorance, that always angered me.

One night early in 1972, soon after I moved to Calgary, I had a particularly disastrous encounter with an inebriated, semi-articulate and memorably offensive expatriate from Glasgow, and I went home fuming about the state of the Scots nation's ignorance about Burns and his work. My wife, God bless her, as is her wont to this day, refused to listen to my ranting and challenged me to put whatever I wanted to say in writing if I thought it was worth saying at all; even then she knew how to shut me up and keep me out of her way for a while.

I collected every book on Burns that I could find in the libraries of Alberta—27 volumes is the number I remember, and they included the two brilliant studies by Hans Hecht and David Daiches—and vanished into the prairies, to a cabin owned by my friend Harold Forster. There, somewhere around the Alberta–Saskatchewan border, I remained alone for almost five weeks, working at all hours of the day and night and completely fascinated by the job I had undertaken and the place in which I was doing it. In my mind, prairie was prairie—vast, oceanic expanses of rolling grasslands, and Saskatchewan epitomized every notion I had. But the location in which I found myself was a serene and secluded valley among rolling hills, fed by a meandering creek and choked with massive and magnificent cottonwood trees—the only stand of trees within miles.

I eventually returned to civilization with a one-man stage show that I had not intended to write—I had set out only to write an essay, a dissertation that would permit me to voice my beliefs and vent my frustrations. But I ended up with a portrait of the man, a retrospective that allowed me to portray Robert Burns in a manner I thought was both accurate and defensible, one I felt might make the poet and his poetry (with its 200-year-old obsolete language) understandable and intelligible to non-Scottish audiences. I performed the show, which I called *Rantin', Rovin' Robin—A Night With Robert Burns*, in most of the major theatrical venues across Canada, until I finally had to stop doing it because of my age (20 years older than Burns at his death).

Remarkably, however, given all my hours on stage and the experiences that emanated from my life as Robbie Burns, the most memorable element of that entire undertaking goes back to those days of reading, thinking and scribbling notes in and around Harold's tiny, mouldering log cabin, on a quiet corner of the property, at a bend of the creek. Harold told me the cabin had once housed the first North West Mounted Police constable who worked in that area, and I was entranced to see some antique equipment, including an anvil and a rusty pair of old handcuffs, still lying among the long rank grass to the right of the cabin door. And thus began my fascination with the horsemen of the original North West Mounted Police.

It was soon after I returned to Calgary with my new show that building in Calgary *really* took off, more intensively from year to year until people joked that the construction crane had been named the official bird of Calgary. High-rise buildings were springing up everywhere, mushrooming in the tightening streets of the downtown centre, and there was a sense of heady excitement everywhere as the first residential twin-tower developments began to rise up in the west end. Beverley and I were among the first residents to move into the 22nd floor of the Place Concorde on 9th Street SW, and from our balcony high above the city we felt like plutocrats.

City Lights

Rectangular lanterns
in thousands,
glistering, crystalline,
frozen
on the gelid anthracite
of February's sky.
Night in the city
in the heartland
of the West;
the continental climate
and the cold:

the deadly, choking,
lung-cracking
nostril-riming
hoary, horrid cold.
Some love the winter
for its powder snow:
the skiers.
Some love the smoothness
of wind-polished ice:
the skaters.
Some hate the rigor mortis
of the frigid dark:
the butterflies.
I would gladly trade
a month of glittering
tinsel-spattered snow-scapes
for one day,
one single afternoon
of floating naked
on a drifting raft;
would exchange
the gaudy Borealis lights
for three short hours
of summer twilight.
From my window
I see windows,
frosted, inanimate,
suspended in the sky;
no shape, no silhouettes,
just windows
painted on the winter sky
like lanterns
by the thousand.

In the autumn of 1973 I was asked by my friend Morris MacFarlane
if I would propose one of the toasts at the annual Robbie Burns Supper at

the Royal Canadian Legion in Lethbridge on January 25. All such events typically feature a tribute to the Immortal Memory of Burns and several toasts, including a toast to the lassies, as Burns is renowned and revered as a superlative lyricist in the writing of beautiful songs to the women he knew and loved; and (everywhere but in Scotland, that is) a toast to the Twa' Lands (two lands,) which endorses the union between Scotland and the land in which the celebrating immigrants happen to be living. In my case, the task was to celebrate the connection between Scotland and Canada.

It turned out to be a daunting and discouraging endeavour, because I soon became convinced that there was nothing I could really say with conviction about Canada that had not been said already by far better and more eloquent speakers than me. I had listened with awe to Tommy Douglas, the former Saskatchewan premier and renowned socialist, proposing the toast to the Immortal Memory the previous year, in Edmonton, and had felt humbled by his insight and his eloquence. And so I floundered around, getting nowhere—an affliction that always seems to assail me as deadlines approach—while time passed with frightening rapidity and the big date, January 25, 1974, approached inexorably. Then one night about a week before the dinner, as I was sitting at home and trying not to succumb to panic, I got thinking about the absence of "wows" from Canadians that I had noticed since setting foot in Alberta, and about my conclusion, back in 1967, that they needed an outsider's eyes to enable them to see what a treasure trove of a country they have here. With that thought having resurfaced, one thing led inevitably to another.

I had been working for several months at that time on putting together my one-man presentation on the life of Burns and had been thoroughly steeped in his work for more than a year, learning by heart dozens of his poems, including most of his long ones and his greatest,

"Tam O' Shanter," and that night I sat staring at the introduction to a poem he had sent to the Earl of Breadalbane, in which he referred to a group of Highlanders who had "fled to the wilds of Canada in search of that fantastic thing—Liberty." Liberty, I realized then, was what I had found in this country—the liberty to be myself, beholden to no one's expectations but my own. It was a freedom I had never known in Scotland, or in England, either. What then, I wondered, might have been Burns' own reaction had he been privileged enough to visit Canada and see it for himself? And so I set out to describe to Burns, using his own verse form from "Tam O' Shanter," the benefits that had accrued to both Scots and Canadians from his day to present times. I wrote the poem in two 45-minute sessions on consecutive evenings and called it "A Toast to Canada, Our Adopted Land."

It was supposed to be a one-off thing; an eight-minute speech (although it turned out to be a poem) about why I loved my adopted land, written for a gathering of about 80 people, mostly Scots and their spouses, at a small-town Burns Supper. But it didn't work out that way. Bob Sharp, a gifted artist and close friend who specialized in formal scrolls and illuminated documents, drove down with me from Calgary to Lethbridge that night and attended the dinner, and when he heard the piece, and witnessed the reaction it generated, he offered to produce and decorate the verse on vellum paper, creating a full-colour visual masterpiece. He did as promised, producing a gorgeous, full-colour, illuminated manuscript on hammered white vellum that would have been worthy of inclusion in a medieval monastic library. People clamoured for copies, but the cost of reproducing the original was prohibitive, and so we printed a less elaborate version, a parchment scroll. Over the next two decades I sold close to 20,000 copies of the piece, worldwide. On three separate occasions over the following eight years, I recited the piece in Toronto at the Canadian National Exhibition's Scottish World Festival, standing alone on the field before thousands of people each night. Today, some 33 years after writing it, I am still asked to recite it for special events and occasions, and I still choke up on parts of it. My feelings about the subject matter have not changed since I wrote the poem, and it speaks for itself.

A Toast to Canada—Our Adopted Land

Tonight I shall propose a toast
To our adopted land, the host
To multitudes of every race
Assembled on the world's great face;
This country, huge, alive and free
And bountiful to you and me
And anyone who wants to stand
Unfettered in a growing land.

But where to begin? I pondered long.
This country where we now belong
Demands so much of a writer's skill,
I might write for a month and still
Not touch on some important part
Of Canada, so where to start?
Here was a problem might indeed
Make even great Rob Burns scratch his heid.

But taking thought, I made the choice
Of ordering my mind, my voice,
To underline and emphasize
The contributions, great in size,
That came straight from old Scotland's hands
To cultivation of this land,
Making of it, from coast to coast,
A home of which proud men can boast.

Our ancestors of auld lang syne

Roamed free among Scotland's heath and pine
'Til the cruel blast of England's power
Deprived them in an evil hour
Of croft and shieling, loch and glen,
Calling them cattle, less than men,
And shipped them off, beyond the seas,
To die, or flourish as they pleased.

Aye, dispossession. Let us now
Return to that sad days, and how
Our ancestors, seasick and sore
Were landed on a foreign shore.
They looked around them, stretched their legs
Shook the wrinkles from the philabegs
And straightway started to command
This country they called "New Scotland."

From Nova Scotia, round the Banks
Of Newfoundland, the Scottish ranks
Spread inwards, aye, and westward, 'til
They crossed one last, majestic hill
And wow, they saw an unco sight!
The great Pacific stretched its might.
Thousands of miles, they'd made their way
Across this land, our home today . . .

Now, some might think I make too much
Of the effect that Scotland's touch
Had on proud Canada's demesne,
But it can be heard, felt and seen . . .
Just let the doubter take a look
At place names on a trip he took,
Or let him ask of one who knows
MacGregors who are Eskimos!

The Fraser and MacKenzie proud;
Selkirk, Calgary, Fort MacLeod;
Banff, Airdrie and Barrhead, now these

Names hardly could be called Chinese!

But influence is reciprocal
And Scots reaction typical,
For though in heart and soul he hold
Heritage and tradition bold,
The Scot is ably born somehow
To love the land he lives in now,
To grow with it, uphold its name,
To work to bring it wealth and fame;
To mix with folk from other lands
To build a nation new and grand;
And Nova Scotians, fierce Acadians,
Take honour in the name Canadian!

Oh, Robert Burns, could you but see
This mighty and superb country,
I think your Muse would hide her heid,
So great would be your bardic need
To capture, with an image terse,
A different scene in every verse,
For here's a country that demands
Fair play, Rob, at the poet's hands.

Great fields, so big, sir, that your plough
Would be worn out, ere you were through.
Great, empty wastes, barren and bare
As poor old Holy Willy's Prayer;
Great, vasty waters, inland seas,
And forests, sir, with mighty trees
That rooted and were growing long
Before you heard the blackbird's song.

And up 'til now, I've said no word
About the creatures, beast and bird,
That make their homes in this great land,
Were never seen on Scottish strand:
Great horned beasties, weird and droll;

Wild animals would scare a foal;
Beasts few men see, names all men know:
Wolf, beaver, bear and buffalo;

Elk, cougar, coyote, caribou
And others would mean nought to you—
Though you might fear for your ain hoose
On meetin' a Canadian moose . . .
They've all roamed here since time began,
Together with the Indian.
Proud peoples of the plains and woods
And Inuit in fur-lined hoods.

Here is a country that the Lord
Has sculpted with a divine sword
A land where man and beast and clime
Conjoin, to give new life to Time;
A land of lands; a place whose worth
Has no peer anywhere on earth;
A land to have; a land to hold;
A land more dear than Pluto's gold.

What more to do? What more to say?
Let me propose a toast
To this land where we are today
This land that is our Host:
Each lad and lass, lift up your glass
And let your mind's eye roam
Across the country, proud and vast,
Our Canada, our home.

From then on, in the early 1970s and right through until 1981, life in Calgary was a roller-coaster ride that I would hate to have missed. Calgary was a boom town, and everything about the city reflected its buoyancy, enthusiasm and incredible resilience. I somehow found myself in the advertising business, as a copywriter and later as a creative director, and discovered that it was no greater a change from entertaining than entertaining had been from teaching. They were all three primarily concerned with storytelling and capturing people's attention, despite their unwillingness to be attracted. And so, until the National Energy Program came along and put an end to the Alberta oil boom in the early 1980s, I worked as a professional scribe and storyteller in Calgary's advertising business, trying to do my best and to maintain my integrity within an industry that was not always conducive to such things.

Song For A Lucky Ad Man

Hey, how can you be creative when there's someone
    right behind you talking shop?
When the phones are going crazy and you're waiting
    for the other shoe to drop?
When your secretary's telling you your invoices are wrong
    and there's a tax inspector going through your books
And you're wishing you were lying in a sauna full of silence
    with a million phones all dangling off their hooks?

There's a fellow hanging round the outer office
    with a sample case that's full,
And another guy who wants to sell subscriptions
    to a merchandising school;
There's an up and coming student, starry-eyed and full of hope
    who just knows that Advertising means romance,
And she only wants a minute or an hour of your time
    so she can talk you into giving her Her Chance!

There's a radio rep. keeps calling 'cause he knows
    your clients need his station's care,
'Cause if they're not on his wavelength,
    they're just wasting money being on the air,
And there's two fast operators, out to make a million Now!
    and they'll share the profits with you, if you're game

Just to let them use your money, credit, time, gifts and know-how,
    plus your talents, reputation and good name.

Ah, the Advertising Business! It's the greatest in the world
    to the armchair-dreaming, would-be Ad-Exec,
But if he had any notion of the toenails it has curled
    or of the ulcers it has spawned he'd yell, "Raincheck!"
For the best thing he could do is change the channel on his set,
    get out his guitar, and relax and sing the Blues
And forget his foolish longings for the glossy-paper set
    with their expense accounts, their models, and their booze:

For it all boils down to working when the damned ideas
    inside your head won't flow
While interruptions and distractions and
    extraneous interactions come and go;
And you know things would be better if your office were a tent
    and you were in it all alone and far from here.
But you know that's wishful thinking, so you smile and you relent
    and you perform and meet your deadlines, year by year.

One of my most memorable times during that period occurred when I was commissioned by someone from Esso Resources to write a poem for one of the company's major suppliers. This was an unusual project for me, because it was to be a corporate gift from Esso Resources in Calgary to the UK-based Luscar Coal Company in Edmonton, to mark Luscar's 225th anniversary. By this time I had been the bard of both the Calgary Burns Club and the Calgary Highlanders Regiment for several years and was widely known on the Calgary entertainment scene for reciting and dedicating the pieces I had written for the two organizations. I had also toured across Canada with *Rantin', Rovin' Robin* and I had received a great deal of attention, both nationally and in the Scots-Canadian community worldwide, for the poem "A Toast To Canada." I can only presume it was a conjunction of those things that resulted in the Esso Resources people's decision to approach me, but once I had accepted the commission and begun to research the task at hand, I found echoes and associations resonating inside me that I had not known were there.

I was born into a small-coal mining community in Scotland, in the county of Lanark, right in the heart of the Lanarkshire coalfields, and grew up steeped in the lore, traditions, history and tribulations of the Scottish miners, or colliers, as they were known. Here I was now, in my mid-30s, discovering that the Luscar Coal Company had begun in Scotland two centuries earlier, and that many of my direct ancestors had worked in Luscar mines. I had grown up amid the detritus of 200 years of mining, when there were abandoned slag heaps, long overgrown with weeds, in every farmer's field. They were called bings or tips, according to where you lived, but even then, in the mid-'70s with the Scottish coalfields shutting down and tens of thousands of miners losing their livelihood, there was a move afoot to clean up the mess and get rid of the bings. I could hardly believe it when I heard or read about it, but it was true. The last time I went home to the village where I grew up, in 2004, there wasn't a bing to be seen anywhere. The countryside had been cleaned up; all the fields were perfectly flat. The slag had been hauled away and processed into tarmac and other paving or building materials. The countryside had been cleansed of the bruises and blemishes that had blighted it all my life, and I missed them. Go figure, as they say.

Reclamation, I learned, was what Luscar Coal now prided itself upon; after one of its mines or open pits was exhausted, Luscar left behind not the slightest sign that a coal-mining operation ever existed there. And so I wrote the poem, and it was appropriately inscribed in black on a sheet of hammered white vellum and presented to the Luscar Coal Company. It hangs in the company's Edmonton head office to this day.

Luscar Coal Company

To the children of Lanark, growing in summer warmth,
The slag heaps were known as bings:
Places of wonder, fairy built; gentle hills
Constructed for childish pleasures.
> They were green clad and climbable,
> Gently contoured, warm in the sun,
> Hospitable in summer months;
> Ignored amid winter's wetness.
But each child knew that underneath
The lushness of the springy, dark green grass
The bings were black—coal black.

To the old men of Lanark, dozing in summer warmth
The slag heaps were known as bings:
Places of memories; symbols of what had been;
Constructed of years of labour.
> They were man made; hand built;
> Shaped out of refuse torn from the living earth,
> Black as the darkness deep beneath the ground;
> Fashioned of toil and sweat.
But each old miner knew that underneath
The muttered curses for a life spent down the pit
There lay pride—coal pride.

> And yet few who looked at the verdant, growing skin
> Shielding the slag heaps' blackness, dark as night,
> Saw any cycle finish or begin.
> Few were the eyes that saw beyond their sight;
> Fewer the minds that grasped the wheel's slow spin;

> For the sky high wheels that held whole towns in sway
> When the black slag heaps were growing to their prime
> Reversed time's cycle in the strangest way,
> Bringing old forests, rich from another time,
> To blaze like a newborn bride in the light of day.

II

To the miners of Luscar, sweating at the deep coal face,
The slag heaps were known as tips:
Headstones to effort; testaments to toil;
Constructed of their workings.
    They were thrown into sunlight,
    Bathed and washed down by sweet, pure, gentle rain;
    Taking up open space in the world above
    To leave room for the men below.
But each Luscar miner knew that underneath,
Down there where he chipped and hacked in his narrow space,
There was power for a growing need—coal power.

To the aesthetes, posturing proud in the public eye,
The slag heaps were known as sins:
Troublesome eyesores; ugly piles of dirt
Marring the landscape's beauty.
    Affronts to artistic temperament, they stood
    Stark, squat; obscene reminders of the lust for power,
    Spoiling the idyll of the leisured class
    That never had to scrabble in the ground.
But each aesthete knew that underneath
The moral revulsion felt in his outraged soul
The need was still there—for coal.

    And so the great search was started for compromise;
    A way to allow each group to achieve its goal;
    The one to preserve the land and the way it lies,
    The other to persevere in the quest for coal,
    And the term Reclamation contained, for each one, the prize.

    So Luscar today can look out and about with pride
    At the places its mines and its men and its workings have been,
    And perceive nothing ugly, no festering sores to hide;
    No scars, no convulsions, no blemishes black, obscene:
    But parkland, and pastures, and croplands rolling and wide.

THIRD-DEGREE BURNS

III

To the tourists, passing Luscar in summer warmth,
The slag heaps have no name:
They are unthought of; they do not exist.
Coal mines are wonders, in and of themselves;
> Things of efficient beauty, they live their now brief lives
> Healthily, quietly, giving offence to none,
> And signals of reclamation are obvious,
> Living beside the works.

Nor does each tourist know that underneath,
When the soil is back in place and the trees take root,
The stone that contained the black of night
And the light of day will be gone,
Leaving forests to grow—coal green?

As always, however, when you start thinking about old times and the things you saw and lived through, endured and enjoyed, it's the people who leap out at you and fill up your reminiscences. One of my favourite poems from those days in Calgary was written in celebration of a family that befriended Beverley and I soon after we stopped living in hotels and became bona fide Calgary residents, paying rent like reg'lar folks and beginning to discover that as "straight citizens" we did not know a lot of people. John and Betty Stein, immigrants to Alberta from Regina, Saskatchewan, had settled in Calgary shortly before we arrived there. They had a family of five—three sons and two daughters—and they took us under their wing and introduced us to all their friends. John was a high-profile lawyer, and Betty one of those women who was born to be a gracious, gifted and wholly natural hostess. Many years later, when they celebrated their 40th wedding anniversary, it was my pleasure to write a poem for them. Some readers may recognize the feel of this piece, for it is a parody of one my favourite comedic songs of all time: Noel Coward's "Mad Dogs and Englishmen."

BALLAD TO LUSCAR

O the children of Luscar, growing in summer warmth
The slag heaps were known as "tips":
Places of wonder, fairy built; gentle hills
Constructed for childish pleasures.
They were green-clad and climbable,
Gently contoured, warm in the sun.
Hospitable in the summer months;
Ignored amid winter's wetness.
But each child knew that underneath
The lushness of the springy, dark green grass
The tips were black - coal black.

To the old men of Luscar, dieing in summer warmth
The slag heaps were known as "tips":
Places of memories; symbols of what had been.
Constructed of years of labour.
They were man made; hand built:
Shaped out of refuse torn from the living earth.
Black as the darkness deep beneath the ground,
Fashioned of toil and sweat.
But each old man knew that underneath
The muttered curses for a life spent down the mine
There lay a pride - coal pride.

But few who looked at the verdant, growing skin
Shielding the slag heap's blackness, dark as night,
Saw any cycle finish or begin.
Few were the eyes that saw beyond their sight:
Fewer the minds that grasped the wheel's slow spin.
Yet the sky-high wheels that held whole towns in sway
When the black slag heaps were growing to their prime
Reversed Time's cycle in the strangest way,
Returning forests, rich from another time,
Once more to the light of day.

To the miners of Luscar, sweating at the deep coal face,
The slag heaps were known as "tips":
Headstones to effort, testaments to toil
Constructed of their workings.
They were thrown into sunlight;
Bathed and washed down by sweet, pure, gentle rain,
Taking up open space in the world above
To leave room for the men below.

But each miner knew that underneath,
Down there where he chipped and hacked in his narrow space,
There was power for a growing need - coal power.

To the aesthetes, posturing proud in the public eye,
The slag heaps were known as sins:
Troublesome eyesores; ugly piles of dirt
Marring the landscape's beauty.
They were affronts to artistic temperament,
Stark, squat, obscene reminders of the lust for power,
Spoiling the idyll of the leisured class
That never had to scrabble in the ground.
But each aesthete knew that underneath
The moral revulsion felt in his outraged soul
The need was still there - for coal.

NO so the great search was started for compromise;
A way to allow each group to achieve its goal.
The one to preserve the land and the way it lies,
The other to persevere in the quest for coal.
And the term "Reclamation" contained, for each one, the price.
So Luscar today can look out and about with pride
At the places its mines and its men and its workings have been.
And perceive nothing ugly, no festering sores to hide:
No scars, no convulsions, no blemishes black, obscene:
But parklands, and pastures, and croplands rolling, and wide.

To the tourists passing Luscar in summer warmth
The slag heaps have no name:
They are unthought of; they do not exist.
Coal mines are wonders, in and of themselves,
Things of efficient beauty, living their now brief lives
Healthily, quietly, giving offence to none.
And signals of reclamation are obvious,
Living beside the works.
And each tourist knows that underneath,
When the soil is back in place and the trees take root,
The stone that contained the black of night
And the light of day
Will be gone,
Leaving forests to grow - coal green.

Jack Whyte · Calgary Alberta · June 1985 · Scott Charism Brown

Thank God for John and Betty Stein

Some people illustrate their life as a race to run
That's why we say they're all workaholic;
No time to contemplate or think about having fun;
No time for leisure, pleasure, or frolic;
From the break of day to the dead of night
They live with a thing called stress
They toil and strain for financial gain
And the trappings of success
They work 'til they drop, cause they just can't stop
In the wind or rain or sun ...
But thank God for Betty and John Stein
and the things they've done.
Some folks will tell you wedding bells are the sound of tears
That nowadays they're pointless, and dated;
And they'll declare that men should all be hung by the ears—
They're polygamous even when mated!
They'll quote you quotes about sowing wild oats
And the tomcat in all men;
Most men today, they will snidely say,
On a scale of one to ten,
Are as prone to cheat as to eat red meat
And reduce all their wives to tears ...
So thank God for John and Betty Stein
And their forty years!
Some people can't see any pleasure in parenthood,
They think their lifestyle might be restricted,
And they'll grow antsy if you even suggest they should
Consider that it's not as depicted.
At the very thought of a tinkling tot
They shudder and shake their head.
And a screaming child can drive them wild
And fill up their hearts with dread;
They can see no need to extend their breed
And that might be well and good,
But thank God for Betty and John Stein
And their healthy brood!

106

Some people sage today still worship eternal youth
In spite of all their talk about "Boomers"
And middle age today is viewed as being quite uncouth
It smacks of whalebone corsets and bloomers!
So we've come from the Coast to propose a toast,
To the two best friends we own;
To the love and the wealth and the ongoing health,
And the happiness they've shown;
To the life they live, and the joy they give,
To their dignity and youth,
And thank God for John and Betty Stein!
Isn't that the truth?

In Yellowknife, celebrating the centennial of the Royal
Canadian Mounted Police's arrival in the NWT

CHAPTER SIX

MOUNTIES

I first saw a real Mountie in Edmonton in the winter of 1967, and I was disappointed at how mundane he looked: against all logic, I had been expecting to see him in a red serge tunic, flat-brimmed Stetson and spurred riding boots. My favourite uncle, an engineering officer in the merchant navy, had brought back from one of his Canadian voyages in the late '50s a black-and-white snapshot showing an RCMP officer, wearing a massive old buffalo-hide greatcoat, directing traffic at an accident scene in some snowbound prairie town, and that image had been engraved into my memory. Of course, by the time I got to Canada 20 years later, those greatcoats were no more, and apart from its wide yellow hatband, the hat of the Mounties' everyday uniform looked to me to be little different from any other copper's anywhere.

I may have felt let down on that occasion, but my fascination with the image of the fabled horsemen had barely begun by then. When I was invited 36 years later to be the guest speaker at the RCMP regimental dinner in Yellowknife, in celebration of the 100th anniversary of the force's arrival in the North West Territories in 1903, I was more than conscious of the honour being extended to me. I wore my full Highland regalia that evening, and I mention it only because I am not used to being out-peacocked when I wear the kilt, but frankly, on that occasion I felt about as sartorially distinguished as a stray strand of kelp, awash on a sea of red serge and gold braid. The term "red tide" has had a special meaning for me ever since that night; I will never forget the sense of pride and esprit de corps that I witnessed there at that centennial gathering.

By 1975 I had been living in Calgary for almost six years and had developed a following sufficient for me to make a stab at putting on a concert, in the 2,700-seat Jubilee Auditorium in Calgary as part of the city's centennial celebration. In defiance of the doubters who asked why people should pay money to see me in concert at the Jubilee when they could hear me for the price of a drink any night of the week, I hoisted my nose in the air, hired a sextet of the best studio musicians in Calgary and staged the concert myself, also producing an elaborate souvenir program, designed and laid out by Bob Sharp. The concert was called "Scotland The Brave—A Salute to the Memory of Colonel J.F. Macleod and the Founding of the City of Calgary, on the Occasion of its Centennial." We filled all 2,700 seats.

A few weeks before the event, when I was researching the history of Calgary and its environs, I had stood on a bluff just outside Medicine Hat, looking down at the site of the infamous Fort Whoop-Up, the illicit whisky-running trading post that the Mounties shut down when they arrived in Alberta. The original wheel ruts dug by the wagons supplying the site with firewater and trading goods are still there, clearly visible from the bluff. Once again I was struck and thrilled by the incontrovertible evidence of how new this country is, and how recently its history was laid down.

There really isn't much to see at the fort other than those old wheel ruts, but the sight of them got me thinking about the calibre and temperament of the original lawmen of Canada's west, and in particular about Colonel Macleod, the impressive man who led the new force into the lands of the Blackfoot Confederacy and who named Calgary after an old estate on his home island of Skye in the Scottish Hebrides. I stopped near the banks of the Oldman River, where the Mounties had first wintered, and visited modern-day Fort Macleod on my way back to Calgary. I did some more digging and discovered that despite widespread awareness of his name throughout southern Alberta, Lieutenant-Colonel James Farquharson Macleod deserves far more commemoration and acknowledgement than we accord him. Everyone in Calgary knows the Macleod Trail, and many know that the town of Fort Macleod, about 100 miles south, is home to a reconstructed fort that honours the origins of the Mounties, but hardly anyone today knows who James Macleod was and what he did for Alberta and western Canada.

I discovered that he had adopted his clan emblem, a black bull's head, as his own personal symbol, which led to his Indian name, Stamix Otokan—literally, Black Bull's Head. Red Crow, chief of the Blood First Nation, a signatory of the Blackfoot Treaty in September 1877, said of Macleod, in the records of that occasion, "Three years ago, when the Mounted Police came to my country, I met and shook hands with Stamix Otokan at the Belly River. Since that time, he has made me many promises and has kept them all. Not one of them has been broken. Everything that the Mounted Police have done has been for our good. I trust Stamix Otokan and will leave everything to him. I will sign with Crowfoot." A couple of days later I wrote the poem "Macleod."

Macleod

Who was this man they call Macleod?
Why should his name resound aloud?
What did he do that makes men proud
   to share his legacy?
With what great gifts was he endowed
   that shaped his destiny?

They called him "Stamix Otokan"
This dour, unbending, upright man
Who bore the standard in the van
   of Justice to the West
And never faltered, never ran
   from any test.

One hundred years ago last year
He and his men arrived out here,
Their mission and their duty clear:
   "Uphold the Right,"
And brought the law that none might fear,
   Red man or white.

Fort Whoop-Up was the biting name
Of that wild place to which they came,
These men in red, to end the game
   profane and loud
That dealt this country bitter shame—
   before Macleod!

The whiskey traders' day was dead
When first they saw the black bull's head
That looked them in the eye and said
   "Go, and be quick,
And let the land grow strong instead
   of pale and sick."

The Indian chiefs, serene and proud
Spoke trustingly of James Macleod,

"Black Bull's Head—Stamix Otokan" and vowed
                    to keep the peace,
Blood, and Blackfoot, with bold Macleod's
                    Mounted Police.

Soldier, diplomat, man of law,
He won respect and earned the awe
That still surround his name, although
                    long years have passed
Since the September day that saw
                    him breathe his last.

Speak highly, then, of James Macleod;
Make sure his name resounds aloud;
His gifts were great, his spirit proud,
                    his word was true
And this great country he endowed
                    to me and you.

Fifteen years after that, by some process of warpage, I suppose, I
found myself writing about the force again, this time from a different,
more reactionary perspective. In "Turbans," I disagreed strongly with
the commonly held viewpoint that Sikh members of the force not
be allowed to wear a turban instead of the traditional flat-brimmed
Stetson. That issue has long since been resolved, but at the time it
caused a lot of upheaval and brought forth a great deal of impassioned
rhetoric, much of which, it appeared to me, was firmly rooted in
racism and xenophobia.

Raised as I was in the last days of the British Raj, and steeped
in the history and traditions of the Empire, I took issue with the
form of the protest—with the concealment of the real issue behind
the hat furor—without commenting too pointedly on its substance.
The force's headgear had been changed before, from the pillbox hat

to the Stetson, and then from the Stetson to the flat-peaked cap. The poem I wrote reflected my opinion that, given the track record of excellence attained by Sikh regiments in India and elsewhere in two world wars, there should be no question of ability or tradition attached to the issue. I think the poem speaks for itself, and my opinion on the matter has not changed.

Turbans

Now, let's look at this new problem that's been causing such a fuss;
This furor about the turban and the things it does to us;
And be truthful; Can the tunic of the Mounties take disgrace
From the head gear that surmounts a dark and bearded Mountie's face?
Stop and think! Think back to India. The British Empire there
Clad its armies in bright scarlet uniforms beyond compare,
And beside the white, pith helmets, underneath the broiling sun
Stood the fierce Sikhs in their turbans, taking second place to none!

They are warriors, these people, with a fierce and noble pride;
Their loyalty is legend and their sense of duty wide;
Sikh Havildars and Sirdars, all in turbans, wore the badge
Of the greatest fighting regiments within the British Raj.
But now, today, they're different, aren't they? Isn't that true?
They won't take off their turbans, and they should! Well, wouldn't you?
Sure, of course you would; at least you might, unless, mind you, you'd checked
And discovered it would cost you every ounce of self respect.

If you found out, say, that taking off your hat would leave you nude
And would demolish the convictions you have held as right, and good;
If you knew that just by taking off your hat you would insult
Every decency you honoured, what conclusions might result?
Could you spurn your own religion? Split your family in strife?
Or humiliate your parents? Could you do that to your life?
Or would you say "The hell with it. If it boils down to that,
They can have their damned police force, yeah! and let them keep their hat!"
The Mounted Force is honoured far and wide and draws recruits

For the scarlet tunic and the yellow stripe; the high, brown boots;
But the Mountie by the roadside doesn't wear the fancy hat;
He's a copper, with a job to do, and he's the best at that.
He's an honourable member of a proud, respected corps
That once stood out, distinguished by the scarlet serge it wore,
He's professionally trained, the best, with or without a hat,
He's Canadian. He's one of us and that, my friends, is that!

Simplicity and modern basics, 1996. *"The Moving Finger writes; and, having writ, Moves on . . . And writes another bit."* (with apologies to Omar Khayyám)

CHAPTER SEVEN

ON WRITING

O ne of the questions I am asked most frequently is, "How did you get into writing in the first place, and was it difficult?" Unfortunately, my answer often provokes raised eyebrows, because people don't expect to hear what I tell them, and their skepticism is sometimes obvious. Be that as it may, my answer remains unchanged: I became a writer almost by accident. True, the inevitability of my eventual career seems obvious now. But during my first few years in Canada, the thought of becoming an author, or even a writer of any description, never even entered my head. I did write poetry then, but purely for my own amusement, to keep my personal predilections for philology and grammar alive and supple. What I wrote, in the main, was narrative verse, the poetic form with which I grew up in Scotland, my love of it having been fed and nurtured by a society that still clings to the oral Celtic tradition within which everyone, irrespective of rank or station, has the right to stand up and perform.

It wasn't until 1975 that I made the serendipitous discovery that would launch me on what I thought of at the time as a "writing binge." I had an idea in my mind to write a story that would solve a riddle that had baffled people for centuries, and provide a feasible explanation of the central mystery of the legend of King Arthur, for I had suddenly become convinced that I knew how the drawing of the sword from the stone by the young king-to-be had been arranged and carried out. In my mind, it was clearly one of the greatest promotional coups of all time, carefully staged and brilliantly managed, and there was not a modicum of supernatural magic involved in it. And so I set out to write the story, secure in the knowledge that I had a great ending.

I did not know that I had yet to find a starting point from which everything could develop logically and naturally, and this quest eventually took me back more than four generations, to the world of two men called Publius Varrus and Caius Britannicus, professional Roman officers in the 20th legion of the army of occupation in Britain toward the close of the fourth century AD. Perfectly content with the basic elements of my tale—the beginning and the ending—I then settled down and wrote in every spare minute I could find for the next 14 years, observing with mild surprise that as my research grew more extensive and specific, I was left with more and more fascinating bits and pieces that cried out to be included in the unfolding tale.

I called the book *The Skystone*, because it was the story of what happened to a stone that fell out of the sky. In writing it, I studied the role of meteoric iron throughout history and learned, in theory, how to make a sword. I also became engrossed in, and almost obsessed by, the various elements and dimensions of the Arthurian legend and how even the most disparate elements could come seamlessly together—for me, at least, as a writer—in the fifth-century collapse of the Roman Empire in the West. I soon had to cut the expanding story into two halves, which became the first two novels of my series *A Dream of Eagles*—and I still had two and a half generations to go.

118

The Legend of the Skystone

Out of the night sky there will fall a stone
That hides a maiden born of murky deeps,
A maid whose fire-fed, female mysteries
Shall give life to a lambent, gleaming blade,
A blazing, shining sword whose potency
Breeds warriors. More than that,
This weapon will contain a woman's wiles
And draw dire deeds of men; shall name an age;
Shall crown a king, called of a mountain clan
Who dream of being spawned from dragons' seed;
Fell, forceful men, heroic, proud and strong,
With greatness in their souls.
This king, this monarch, mighty beyond ken,
Fashioned of glory, singing a song of swords,
Misting with magic madness mortal men,
Shall sire a legend, yet leave none to lead
His host to triumph after he be lost.
But death shall ne'er demean his destiny who,
Dying not, shall ever live and wait to be recalled.

Even then, however, and as late as 1988, when I had three complete 1,000-page manuscripts in hand and was busily working on the fourth, I never thought of myself as an author who would be published. I was writing a story, certainly, but it was a minor obsession of mine and a private, personal thing that only my wife and a few close friends were aware of—a story that was inside me and just had to come out.

The truth is, writing that story—and the entire *A Dream of Eagles* series is really one huge novel—I was continuing a process that had begun when I was in grade school in Scotland, where I first developed what grew into a lifelong devotion to the mechanics of the English language. Some kids are natural mathematicians. Others are natural athletes, and still others are born with an affinity for the sciences or for music. I seem to have been born with an intrinsic love of language, and I was fortunate enough between the ages of eight and eleven to have a series of devoted teachers in grade school—all of them maiden ladies of a certain age, part of that generation of women whose lives were unalterably blighted by the cataclysmic loss of eligible men in the Great War. Long dead now, they would all have been in their late 50s and early 60s and approaching retirement when I was one of their pupils, but they all delighted in the way I sucked up everything they taught me.

They were all "Misses"—Miss Callaghan (Big Mary) Miss Gibson (Wee Betty) and Miss Hughes (Big Aggie)—and for three consecutive years, passing me along from hand to hand, they taught me to revere and enjoy the wonder and the logical majesty of syntax and analysis, of scansion and prosody. They taught me to love and appreciate the way language *works*, how all the various pieces come together to create the magic of great stories and exciting poetry. And they taught me that this love was a gift that I was never to lose. It was a gift, in fact, that I value more highly with each day that passes and with each great book I read. But even then, before I was 11 years of age, my love of language was real and abiding. Syntax was my overriding passion as a preteen boy: for the sheer fun of it, I would open a book at random—any book— and parse a paragraph or an entire page, identifying and defining the various structural properties and parts of speech in every phrase and sentence, and the various clauses of a compound-complex sentence would leap up off the page to demand my attention.

Although it may appear as though I have had several different careers, everything I have done in my adult life has had a direct connection to storytelling in one form or another, and to what I was taught in those early years. It began with singing in folk clubs, morphed into teaching English through Speech and Drama, went on to entertaining as a ballad singer, and then to playwriting, acting, scriptwriting for television, designing and implementing advertising campaigns, and eventually working as communications director for a number of corporations, both public and private. All of this work involved storytelling and writing, getting the message across effectively, seamlessly and convincingly. And yet, in the end, when my books were published, my audience, to my great chagrin, was confused, even if it was a confusion caused by the marketing people at my US publishing house.

The original *A Dream of Eagles* series comprised five novels, but the last of them, *The Sorcerer*, was too long at 1,100 pages to be published as a single book, I was told, and so it was split into two volumes, two exact halves. The first half was to be called *The Sorcerer—Book 1: The Fort at River's Bend* while the second half, to be published no more than three months later, would be *The Sorcerer—Book 2: Metamorphosis*. The publisher of the Canadian version got it right, but the Americans published the first half with no mention of *The Sorcerer*, and that confusion has plagued me ever since, to the point where I will never again consent to having one of my books divided arbitrarily. I just won't write any more that are that long!

So how did I become a *professional* writer? Given my lifelong love of stories and the rules and syntax of the English language, I suppose it was inevitable that I would end up writing full-time, but the fact that I have still surprises me sometimes, even though I know I have an ear and an eye for a good story. God gave me a gift and saw to it that I had a magnificent and unending series of teachers and mentors to guide me along until I could hitch up my pants and strike out on my own, even if I remained blind to what I was doing and where I was headed.

At any rate, I had been writing for 13 years—going on 14—before I even thought about approaching a publisher, because my "story" wasn't finished. It was a project, a work in progress, and something that I just had to get out of me and onto paper. And it was a private thing, for the most part. I didn't talk much about it except with my closest friends, and even they reached the point of wondering whether it was kosher to ask me if I was still "buggering about with that thing in the basement." I mean, 13 years *is* a long time.

But then Beverley suggested that I think about getting the work published, since, irrespective of the fact that the opus was incomplete, I nonetheless had three 1,000-page manuscripts sitting on my shelves. So I decided to give it a go, despite being terrified that someone would come back to me and say, "Sorry, but you've just wasted 13 years of your life on an unpublishable pile of garbage."

Although few people had even known I was writing The Book, the moment I decided to try to have it published hundreds of people emerged from cracks in the woodwork and gaps in the walls, all of them wagging their fingers and shouting, "You can't do that! Who do you think you are? You can't come up out of your basement after 13 years and blithely expect to get published, just like that!" They gave me a thousand perfectly valid reasons why I was living in a fool's paradise and why I should prepare to be annihilated by the critics of the publishing world. One silly woman, whose name is long forgotten but who had served in some supernumerary capacity on the outskirts of the Canada Council, even sat down next to me at a dinner party and said with a condescending sniff, "Well, it's hardly literature, is it?"

I was working in Vancouver at that time, for Johnston Terminals, and had met and become friends with Alma Lee, who was just launching her hugely successful Vancouver International Writers and Readers Festival. She put me in touch with a remarkable lady called Marion Hebb, now legal counsel for the Writers Union of Canada. Through Marion, I was able to present my material to Doug Gibson, then publisher at Macmillan of Canada and only coincidentally a fellow Scot. Doug tried diligently for an entire year to persuade his editorial committee to publish the books, but they were intimidated by the scope of the project—at that time four novels, and by a completely unknown writer. He advised me to take the series to a major international publisher, as the Canadian market was too small for what I was hoping to achieve.

I took his advice and approached Penguin Books. I wrote to a gentleman called Brad Martin, who was at that time vice-president of sales for Penguin Canada. I sent him a brief letter introducing myself, a one-page synopsis of the overall work, and a one-page synopsis and sample chapter of each of the existing novels. He wrote back almost within the week, inviting me to send him what I had, and I fired off all three manuscripts.

I was very lucky—some people would say *unbelievably* lucky. I had found the right man, with the right interests, at exactly the right time, and he decided my work should be published. Be that as it may, when young writers approach me nowadays, careworn and discouraged by the shortcomings of the system, I encourage them to keep going, and to keep rewriting, because I firmly believe that if a book—any book— is *written* well enough, it will find a publisher somewhere. And that even applies to narrative verse, that outmoded, outlandish poetry from another era.

Narrative verse is, of course, rhyming verse—an old-fashioned poetic form, strict and rigid in its construction in accordance with the disciplined rules of rhythm, prosody and scansion. Even the words "prosody" and "scansion" look alien nowadays, seldom seen and certainly never mentioned in polite company. But I learned them in school. They deal with the rhythmic synthesis of verse and rhyme, and they are as exact as hundreds of years of growth and tradition in the English language can make them.

It annoys me intensely when I hear people refer to rhyming verse—always dismissively and scathingly—as *doggerel*. Writing verse is hard work, and the better the verse, the more intense the effort to produce it. Its construction requires a thorough working knowledge of grammar, punctuation, spelling and poetic structure—skills that are seldom or little taught in modern schools. Verse writing also requires discipline and a vocabulary of more than 200 words. When it is successful, the result is delightful and pleasing. Good, strong, fluent verse is invariably a pleasure to read and to hear recited. Doggerel, on the other hand, is plodding, weak, rhythmically unsound, sloppy, predictable and usually embarrassing. Not all verse is doggerel, but all doggerel is, by definition, bad verse.

What I love most of all about narrative verse is that it's fun to write, and this sense of fun is communicable: it shines through, strong and unmistakable, in the finished pieces. Since boyhood, I have had a triumvirate of guides within the world of narrative poetry, one of them a Brit, the second an Australian and the third, and by no means the least of them, a Canadian—well, he was a Brit, actually, but he personifies the Canadian North. They are Rudyard Kipling, Andrew Barton (Banjo) Paterson and Robert W. Service, and their delightful works have frequently provided me with templates for my own efforts. Each of these men is a gifted storyteller with an unerring eye for a great or amusing tale, a wide-ranging and versatile vocabulary, and an absolute mastery of the rules and tenets of writing verse. By studying what they did in their day, I learned how to look for the same kind of things in my own work.

Given that you have a clear understanding of how rhyme and scansion really work, and your vocabulary is eclectic yet accessible and comprehensible to your readership—all you really need is a thought to start you off, an idea to get the ball rolling and set your story in motion. Some people think of that initial thought as an inspiration, the galvanizing spark that leads to creation. I tend to think of it as a hook from which, or on which, I can hang my creative canvas. And the beauty of the whole thing is that once you've begun, there really are no limits to where your mind will take you, or to the form your thoughts will dictate, so long as you have a story with a beginning, a middle and an end. Many people over the years, after reading or listening to the poems I have written, have remarked on the variety and range of what I write. But really, they are all stories, even the ones with a moral or a lesson in them. And one of the most striking of those that I ever wrote—at least in my own estimation—was a little homily-style poem I wrote for my son when he received his majority, as we used to say.

125

I remember turning 21 myself, back in the long ago days, when you got "the key of the door" (the right to vote and live independently), because you were generally acknowledged to be an adult. When I was a kid in Britain, you could drive a car at 18, or be called up for your national army service and get legally killed in a war. You could also walk into any pub in the country and buy beer. But you couldn't vote. That had to wait until you were 21. When I recall how *young* I was at 21, how green and callow and unfit to be let out without a keeper and a chain, I cringe. And then along came the day when my stepson Mitch turned 21, and I had to think of something to say to him. What came out was the poem "For Mitch, at Twenty-One," which also went, with minor changes, to my own son Mike when he reached the same milestone a few years later.

For Mitch, at Twenty-One

Congratulations, Mitch, your first lap's run;
You've left boyhood behind; you're twenty one;
A formal, legal adult, fully grown
And from this day forth, son, you're on your own.
If truth has any worth, it has to be
To your lifelong advantage that you see
Now, at this point, that no one ever cares
About those crises that you can not share.

No one can make your mind up, Mitch, but you.
You must decide what you will be and do;
No other living being on this earth
Can prescribe what you'll be, or what you're worth,
Unless you choose to let someone dictate
Your life's terms, lad. You're free to abdicate,
To give up on your life, waste it away,
Squander tomorrow on a wild today . . .

You alone arbitrate your life's extent.
You'll be the final judge of how you spent
All of your time, and when that judgment's made,
You'll allocate the passing/failing grade.
One life is yours, to do with what you will:
One soul, one mind, one destiny; fulfill
Each one, or squander it? The choice
Is yours and private 'til you give it voice.

And at the end of all, the bottom line
Has to be more concerned with me and mine
Than it can be with yours, his, hers or theirs,
For the unvarnished truth is, no one cares
What you do with your life. "That silly clown!
I've problems of my own! He let me down!"
That's the response you'll earn if things go wrong
For every man must sing his own life's song.

And though that might sound harsh, let truth be told:
Each person who's alive is growing old
And grappling, more or less, with thoughts of death.
No one can breathe with someone else's breath . . .
None feel your pain, experience your fears,
None think your thoughts, hear music through your ears,
See rainbows with your eyes, smile with your lips
Or feel sensations through your fingertips.

As none can know the mind that rules your ways,
So none should think to designate your days.
Take strength from that. Be proud to stand and know
That you are seen to stand, prepared to grow,
Go for your goals, strive for what you desire,
Know what you want, and keep going when you tire;
Weigh your decisions, calculate your chance,
Weigh up the odds and plan far in advance.

But if you fail to find yourself; to vault
Above the norm, Mitch, that will be your fault;
Not mine, your mother's, family's, wife's or friends',
Just yours, and yours alone, and there it ends.
One more truth, son. The older that we get,
The greater grow our fears that we might yet
Fail, or give up, or lose that vital drive
That keeps us viable and makes us strive

To beat, improve upon, revise, update
All that we've done before that's second-rate;
For nothing, ever, that's already done
Should offer half the challenge or the fun
Of what's upcoming, what we have to do
Tomorrow; something still undone, still new;
Something bigger and greater, something fine
That we can look at some day, saying, "That's mine!"

So that's it, Mitchell, that's all my advice

For you to read, consider, say "That's nice,"
And promptly disregard, to carry on
Living your life, setting your foot upon
The next, singular step along the way
To where you're going. I hope, once there, you'll say,
"So far, so good! I'm here, safely arrived,
Whole, unimpaired, unhampered and alive!"

Of course, one birthday is pretty much like another until you become aware of how they're accumulating, and at that point they begin to assume certain significant characteristics. I've never liked being told what to think or what to say, so I eschew traditional birthday cards, preferring to write my thoughts for specific friends, but, like the man said, there comes a time when everyone has to catch the same bus.

Fifty

At twenty-one we know it all,
We're new, we're neat, we're nifty!
We never think of time at all
And can't imagine fifty . . .

At thirty-one we're still brand new,
Living from day to day,
We've deals to make and things to do
And fifty's miles away.

By thirty-five we're in our prime,
Immune to doubts and fears;
Potent, productive, with no time
To check the flitting years.

At thirty-nine we hesitate
And check the looking glass;
Gray hairs! Still, kid, you're looking great
But, God! How time goes past!

At forty-five we stand apart,
Beside Time's swirling river,
Wishing we had some magic art
To keep us there forever,

But forty-six and forty-seven
Come, even though we're thrifty
By now with every hour we're given
And, suddenly, we're fifty!

So, Peter, stay light on your feet!
The sands of time are shifty.
But smile, relax—'cause life is sweet
And you're still only fifty!

During the blackout in wartime Britain, we often had power
outages, caused by bomb damage. They became less frequent after the
initial blitz years of 1940 and 1941, but they never really died out. On
many occasions I would listen, rapt, as the grownups sat around a coal-
oil lamp or single candle, talking in whispers simply because there was
something about the lack of light that demanded voices be kept low. I
have been fascinated ever since by the terrifying hold that darkness has
had over people through the ages. There is nothing more comforting
than a gleam of light when you are in absolute darkness.

A Candle

A candle, bravely banishing the dark
That presses all of us on every side,
Is something we can easily ignore
Until we have dire need of one,
But when the power fails and night falls stark
Over our eyes, then all our pride
In being self-sufficient has no more
Potency than icicles in the sun.

A candle is a promise, and a prayer
That darkness never might invade our lives,
For darkness masks the demons of the night
And threatens us with fears of the unknown;
Fears that once kept our ancestors aware
Of the futility of blunt stone knives
Brandished against the chill absence of light
In places that, by day, were theirs alone.

A candle's light can fill an empty room,
Illuminate a path, and bathe a family's faces;
Its golden warmth can heat a storm-chilled car
Caught in a blizzard, stalled, at point of death.
A single light-source, flickering in the gloom
Of one of life's darkest, despair-filled places,
Marital strife, can show us who we are
And call us back to love, and grant us breath.

It is hard to believe that 20 years have passed since the Exxon Valdez disaster in the pristine waters of Alaska. I had never thought of myself as an environmentalist until I heard on the radio one day some local yokel vocal group singing the most appalling drivel about the environment that I had ever heard. I switched off the radio in disgust, remarking to Beverley that it was little wonder some people painted environmentalists as loonies. Beverley, knowing me better than I knew myself, said, "Look it! If you have anything to say about that, write it down. Don't just sit there waving your finger in my face." So that night, I wrote "The Faceless Ones," which received far more attention than I would ever have anticipated. Terry Jacks, formerly of the Poppy Family and "Seasons in the Sun" fame, now a prominent environmentalist, talked me into recording it, and it eventually won two gold medals, for Best Writing and Best Narration, at that year's New York Festival of Film and Television. People ask me how I wrote it, and even how I thought of it in the first place, and my answer is that I got angry. Anger, passion, enthusiasm—call it what you will, it is always a great initiator of writing.

The Faceless Ones
A Reflection . . .

When the Exxon Valdez spilled her guts
Off Alaska's pristine shore
She belched black shame, spewing bitter blame
For the Faceless to ignore;
But the Valdez trull with her single hull
Wasn't special or unique—
It was just bad luck that the thing got stuck,
To hear the Faceless speak . . .
    Where oil slicks spread the birds are dead—
    Their feathers destroyed by tar;
    The seals are gone; no salmon spawn
    Where the thick, black globules are;
    No whales sound there; no hungry bear
    Will set foot on a black ice floe
    To hunt for food in a sea of crude
    That smothers the life below.

When you drive again through the mountain chain
That makes B.C. so fair,
Look up in awe at the Mackinaw made of trees
That the mountains wear;
And you might take note that the once-thick coat
Is showing wear and tear;
It still looks fine, but the holes are sign
That the Faceless Ones are there.
    When the hills are bare, there'll be no soil there
    For trees to fasten on;
    Just plain, raw rock. The bright woodcock
    Will be vanished; dead and gone.
    There'll be no life there for the grizzly bear;

Neither cougar nor wolf will prowl;
No sign of flight through the woods at night
Will signal the hunting owl.

There's blood in the ooze from the tankers' screws
There's blood in the chain saw's teeth;
There's dread in the thread of the steel cat's tread
The torn earth screams beneath;
There's the breath of death in the pipeline's path
And the strip mine's open sore;
And the pulp mills sweat a cold, poisoned threat
To our children that we can't ignore!
    There's contaminated salmon and poisoned fish
    We've been told are safe to eat,
    And, if caught outside of the grim Red Tide,
    They say mussels can still taste sweet.
    A drop in the ocean is just a drop,
    But its meaning has changed today
    When one toxic drop has the power to stop
    A migrating whale, midway!

These are the gifts of the Faceless Ones,
The ones who will swear, "Not I!"
As they defend to the tasteless end
Their plight and their right to ply.
They'll swear you threaten their livelihood;
That your ignorance is plain;
While, all the time, they produce the slime
That the papers call Acid Rain.
    And they'll tell you that Pontius Pilate's dead;
    That his days, and his ways, are gone . . .
    Did he wash his hands of the Empire's plans
    For the cedars of Lebanon?
    They cut and they squandered the forests there,
    And they shipped the lumber home,
    And the desert sands of the Arab lands
    Are the legacy of Rome . . .

We must take aim at the Faceless Ones
Though they're always hard to find;
They take no blame, but they're all the same,
The blind who lead the blind.
They sit, in power, in ivory towers
And decree how we live our lives;
They throw us bones and honing stones
But they hold the long, sharp knives.
> They'll take no blame for the cancer flames
> That pour through the ozone holes;
> They'll hear no tales about dying whales
> Or ice melting at the Poles;
> They'll disown Bhapal and the Love Canal
> And Chernobyl's grim despair;
> And they'll wash their hands of the blasted lands
> That lie barren, and bleak, and bare.

We must stand up to the Faceless Ones,
The men who control the winds;
The winds of power, and the winds of war
The fiscal, blizzard winds;
The winds that soar and the winds that roar
And the winds that destroy the trees;
We must make them see that the winds of change
Can be stronger than all of these!
> But we might just find that the Faceless kind
> Look a lot like you and me,
> Though they're ill-defined . . . there are none so blind
> As those who will not see . . .
> And so, when the trace of the shadowy face
> You're straining to see has grown,
> Don't stand and stare if the features there
> Are very much like your own.

For we, ourselves, are the Faceless Ones
Though we might find that uncouth . . .
We've grown too fond of the easy life

In our hunt for Eternal Youth.
We've grown accustomed to reaching out
For whatever we want, right now,
Never stopping to think that you just can't drink
Fresh milk, once you've killed your cow . . .
>
> So we cut down the forests and foul the air
> And pour filth in our rivers and streams.
> Polluting the oceans, we go through the motions
> Of calling for grandiose schemes
> To save the rain forests and restore the ozone,
> And put the world back in the pink.
> But the thing we won't do, is admit that it's true
> That we'd all better slow down and think!

But anger, passion and enthusiasm can sometimes be replaced and even outstripped by good old humour, especially when it forms the basis for a well-remembered story.

Le Mot Juste

We were arguing one evening, as the sun was going down,
About the names we give to groups: The old Collective Noun.
We had gone through prides of lions; schools of fish; brigades of foot,
When I wondered, "What's collective for the poor old prostitute?"

Well! I felt as though I'd stepped upon a hidden hornets' nest,
For each man proposed an answer, and each swore his was the best!
We'd a treasury of trollops, and a tragedy of trulls;
An entire Who's Who of hookers and a calamity of culls . . .

We'd a pastry cook among us who, in tribute to his arts,
Put forth the obvious image of a tempting tray of tarts,
While a fishmonger there present, who was more than slightly nuts,
Proposed the odious and malodorous catchphrase "a slab of sluts!"

Then our resident militiaman cried out "A troop of tramps!"
But he was shouted down in favour of a vile vendue of vamps;
A convention of solicitors; a haggling horde of whores;

Such invention for the ladies whom society deplores!

No, the task of giving pride of place was not a simple one.
The concubinage of courtesans might easily have won,
Or the hostile hiss of hustlers, but we had to share the rose
Between a bright fanfare of strumpets and an anthology of pros . . .

Other times, you write about deeply felt things because you just don't know what to say, or because you *do* know what you want to say but know no one wants to hear it. The poems "My Friend" and "Funeral" are examples of this, and although they might not appear at first glance to be narrative verse, they really are.

My Friend

Robert is hurting,
aching audibly,
his iron-hard integrity
now breached, deformed,
twisted and wrenched,
warped by a pain like none
he could visualize
in bygone times last year;
Robert was ill-prepared,
unready and unbraced
to stand against the weights
life threw at him
so savagely, so brutally
gauging his weakness.
Either he might have handled.
Both, those specific two, were just too much.
His sturdy shoulders, never bent
through all his working years,
are bowed now, strained,
inwardly sloping, beaten,
to his chest.

Muscle has drained from him,
falling from his weariness,
making his bigness slight.
Robert is ageing visibly,
His losses graven stark
in facial fissures,
sagging folds of skin,
and haunted eyes
riven with shadows that occlude
the soul that shone within him.
Two things had kept him young,
denied the years
and made him vibrant
and both were love:
His Music ¾ his soul's mistress;
and his Mistress ¾ his soul's music.
Losing them both,
almost within the span of one short song
he lost his joie de vivre;
his joy in life and life of joy
are gone,
together at the end.
Now I watch Robert fade
and hate the process and its strength in him;
I see the void in him,
the emptiness, acceptance,
austere pain, and growing, glaring fear
of his mortality;
the acknowledgement of time;
the concession to age
and ageing
and the loss of hope and youth.
Robert has surrendered his resilience.
The bounce has gone from his athletic stride,
withering with his smile.
God! I resent the useless sacrifice
of what made Robert what he used to be:

The Rabelaisian, leering, vulpine grin,
the dancing eyes
the flaring laugh
the raucous, raunchy earthiness
that marked him as unique.
Robert's my friend.
He used to be my mirror.
I miss him when we meet and talk,
For Robert has withdrawn.

Funeral

A funeral, epitomizing death,
is nonetheless a living, sentient thing
during its own brief lifetime,
usurping all awareness to itself,
procreating itself in daylight,
flaunting its one, non-human privilege,
rebirth,
provoking an orgiastic and communal lust
to cleave to life,
stirring the living to reflect, with guilt,
upon the orgasmic brevity of life,
focusing horror on the insecurity
and risk in the midst of being ...
Its catalytic urgency denies
and yet confirms the life force,
thrusting awareness of futility,
of transience, into public view.
It lends a sexuality, directly,
to the virulent and quite improper breeding
of misshapen words and phrases.
A funeral, at best, is a cliché at stud:
progeny gush full-formed from its loins
without need of gestation;
small, jaded phrases, twisted, homunculus,

swarm and expand and, screaming, devour silence,
deafening and deaf, redounding on themselves,
rattling, cacophonous, like jangling skeletons,
filling the emptinesses of unuttered thought
with false appearances of comprehension,
equanimity, compassion and acceptance.
Then talk is all of change and lack of change:
time and some people change
and nothing changes.
None there speak ill of death or of the dead.
Guests move away, around, about, avoiding guests,
avoiding spectral faces, avoiding truth,
talking in nothingnesses of how people move,
discover different interests, make new friends,
lose their old ways, forsake their roots,
deny their past, and die, frightening everyone.
There will be time, they tell themselves,
to readjust, to think things out, tomorrow,
to adjust to life again
tomorrow; things will change
tomorrow; all things change, with time;
nothing remains unchanged, except things dead
and death decrees dire change even to those.
Only in memory, it seems, does non-change lie,
and yet we modify that constantly,
giving our psyche license to transmute
the fact of death into the fantasy,
the half-life, of selective recall.
Few are the dead things people can perceive
just as they were in death.
Live, vibrant things obstruct our view of them.
Grass grows around their edges in our minds.
Distance obscures their colours with a lichen coat
and other things, dead in the interim,
collapse across them, skewing perspective,
cluttering sight lines, hindering access,
creating illusions, warping, cramping,

tunneling, confusing, misleading,
changing the very truth of memory.
A funeral is abrupt, traumatic truth,
forcing our impotence to recognize
omnipotence in death.
And so the clichés are muttered, half articulate,
and the funeral's dying gasps are noted,
prayed for and preyed upon because they mark
the advent of the moment of escape
back into life's short fugue.

There are times, however, when you write about a deeply moving event long after the fact, when you realize the experience won't leave you alone until you purge yourself of how it affected you. That happened to me in the summer of 1975. I was on tour with my Robbie Burns show and had just done a live interview, wearing my Burns costume, on a local Toronto TV station (the name of the show and its host have disappeared from my memory). When I left the set, I was told there was a telephone call for me, and I was surprised because I didn't know a soul in Toronto at that time. I answered the phone and the fellow on the other end said, "Hello, Mr. Whyte. My name's Jinallan Cameron and I've just watched your interview and decided to call you."

I was stunned, because John Allan Cameron—Jinallan, as Maritimers called him—was well known to me. He was to Nova Scotia in those days what Robert Burns had been to Scotland 200 years earlier, and he was an icon to Maritimers everywhere. We talked for some 10 minutes, and when he discovered that I was appearing next at Hamilton Place, he insisted that I check out of my hotel in Toronto and drive out to spend the weekend with him and his wife in London, after which he would drive to Hamilton with me to see me perform. It was impulsive and spontaneous, but the invitation was genuine and I've been glad ever since that I accepted it as reflexively as I did. He and I worked together several times in the years that followed, and I was deeply saddened when he died in 2006. I immediately dug out the poem that I wrote after driving to London to visit him that afternoon.

Ontario Sunsink

A super-nova, blaring stridently,
The sun sinks slowly,
Viscously,
Down the cyclorama of the sky
And assaults me callously,
Finding with huge disdain
The thumb-length gap
Between my guardian visors.
It ricochets from the hood,
Whites out my windshield
And smashes me between the eyes.
Late fall; early evening;
Central Ontario; Highway 401,
Heading west.
Everyone in the world
With an ounce of sense
Is heading east.
Frost and a smear of snow have killed
The geriatric summer.
Colours are muted;
Washed with pale, pale grey.
Moorlands flaunt brassy puddles
Where cold ducks float
Mired in an autumn wasteland of dead leaves.
Shadows slice from the searing, icy sun
In unrelieved incisions,
Blue-black and purple
On the sun-scrubbed moor
Where crags erupt like scabs,
Great dots of blood

Congealed
On the scoured, bleak, blasted face
Of this uncared-for place.
The road is blatant, blazing yellow-grey:
An endless mirror
Throwing the sun's malevolence in my face.
And then a bank,
A turn,
A god-sent shadow
Enables my tense forehead to relax,
Unknot itself, experience ecstasy.
I stretch my facial muscles,
Blink my eyes,
Yawn without yawning
And enjoy the bliss, the dear relief
Of normal vision while the twisting road
Winds round the kindly hillside
And returns
To writhe in howling, squirming impotence
Under the scourging, harsh intransigence
Of the flagellant sun.
The traffic passing in the eastbound lane
Looms molten-edged,
Lambent with blazing chrome
Out of the fire ahead and falls away,
Plunging to normalcy
In the uncluttered unreality
Of the rear-view mirror.
Ahead of me, a truck, Leviathan,
Grim and unyielding, holds the outside lane
And I pull out to pass and then
Rest shamelessly, a purblind succubus,
Glutting upon the hugeness of his shade,
Praying that while I prey on him he too
Will not pull out to pass some other thing.
The image of the sun, a billiard ball
Behind my aching, weary, glare-blind eyes,

141

Seems welded to my temples.
One more inch it has to sink,
In terms of my tormented, tortured view,
Before the kind horizon leaps at it
And spreads a warm red blanket
To engulf its hellish blaze.
The truck rolls backwards
And again I cringe.
Here's a bridge, a valley
And a range of hills
Behind whose swelling breasts
The sun is lost.
And, startling in its brightness,
A golf course, green, voluptuous,
Fresh-manicured,
Spreads its well-tended, cultivated charms
Across the rolling hillside,
Wantonly beckoning, with salacious lust,
Like a luxuriant strumpet.
And in the shallow climb along her side,
Marvelling at the way her thighs seem spread,
And how her trees seem clustered
Just like hairs
A miracle occurs and I emerge,
Wincing and vulnerable upon the hillside's crest,
To find the sun fast-dying,
Gorged with blood,
His searing fury stifled,
His shape, though still a clear-edged billiard ball,
Suffused with crimson: turned from white to red.
And I relax
And breathe a sigh
And switch my headlights on.

In the mid-1980s, when Johnston Terminals Ltd. was approaching
its 75th anniversary, I was contracted to research and write the company's

corporate history. The book was never published, for a variety of reasons, but in the course of my research I discovered all kinds of amazing things about the birth, development and expertise of the company. One image lodged itself in my mind and would not go away: a photograph of young Elmer Johnston, who founded the company in 1913, at the moment of his inspiration, when the vision of what he might do with his life first came to him. It's a true story, and I had no need to exaggerate in the telling of it.

Summer, 1913

Imagine the scene as it might have been
On a summer day in 1913;
The sky clear blue, the ocean green;
Vancouver sparkling in between . . .
A shower had passed and the earth was damp
So you could smell the horses
That stood beside the loading ramp
Relaxing in their courses.

There, in that drab, freight haulage yard
Sacred to Trade and trading,
A young man sat daydreaming, finding it hard
To focus on piled bills of lading,
And the green sap of summer smelled sweet in the air
And the dray horses steamed in the heat
And his job was to be there, to sit and compare
Columns scratched on a dry balance sheet.

Out there in Vancouver he knew—he could feel—
Lay his destiny, rounded and whole;
Shiny, new, bright and personal, solid and real,
And he yearned for it deep in his soul.
But he sat there alone, with a job not half done,
Left behind by the men who employed him
While they lounged out of doors, there, enjoying the sun,
And that basic injustice annoyed him.

He was only a teamster ... not heard, and not seen;
He could quit, and they'd think it no loss;
But he'd thoughts of his own, about what could have been
If he'd just had one chance to be Boss ...
He'd just come to the City, from Ontario,
With a wife and a small baby son
And he hoped that B.C. would allow him to grow
And expand to become a Someone.

144
He'd had breakfast that day, on his way in to work,
With a clever, ambitious young friend
Who was making a fortune—a "coming young turk"—
Building warehouses in the East End ...
He sat up and blinked, sighed, and tried to ignore
Both his thoughts and the sunshine outside
As he picked up his pen and scowled down at the floor;
But the dreams in his head were too wide.

Then the door was flung open. A stranger strode in,
Opportunity, heaven sent,
And he looked at the young man and asked, with a grin,
"Do you guys have space you could rent?"
The young man blinked again, for he knew right then
That the fellow meant warehouse space,
And he knew they had none and he'd just begun
To say "No", when the stranger's face

And the strength in it, the need, the stress,
Told him here was a chance indeed,
And he stopped, and he thought, and he whispered, "Yes,
We might have ... How much do you need?"
"Two thousand square feet; dry, sound and strong;
No dampness—I deal in stoves.
They don't mind dust, but they can't stand rust
And I import them, in droves!"

Elmer Johnston stood up. "I'll know tonight
For sure. Can we meet about ten?"

"Right here," said the stranger, "but don't let me down.
Find me space, and we'll deal again."
Well, it seemed that day would never end,
But before the sun went down
Young Elmer had made a firm deal with his friend
Who built warehouses in town,

And he'd rented a warehouse on Beatty Street;
Two floors—with the upstairs space
Just right for the man with the need to meet
And the stoves to fill the place.
There were two deals here, because Elmer knew
What he'd charge and what he must pay;
And he moved in downstairs as a tenant, too,
Rent free, with a team and a dray.

That's how Johnston Terminals first began;
On young Elmer's dream of a chance
To better himself and become a man
That no one could order to dance!
He remembered that day, and the way he felt
When they told him to stay inside,
And he swore no teamster who worked for him
Would lose dignity or pride.

So he let every man find himself as a man
And be proud, and believe over all
That the knowledge he gained as a Johnston Man
Would allow him to stand up tall.
And so Elmer's name, in the Transport game,
Is remembered even now
By the people he taught—for they never forgot—
That "Johnston" means "Know-how".

Another example of how a story can be hung from a "hook" occurred
to me a short time ago. I was once asked to write some words in honour of

Buck Gibb, a member of the board of directors of an industrial association in Vancouver for which I had done corporate communications work in the early 1990s, and although I originally accepted the task as a PR gesture, I was soon pleasurably immersed in the project. I didn't know Buck personally—I'd seen him only occasionally, sitting down the table from me, listening closely to everything that was being said—but he was clearly well liked by his colleagues. He would be celebrating his 60th birthday soon, and they wanted to do something really special for him, something more meaningful than a stodgy gift presentation. And so I began making the rounds of his colleagues, asking a few questions about him, and I came up with this wonderful story from his younger days.

Buck Gibb and the Cedar Tree

There's a story told when the nights are cold
To the north of the Lions Gate Bridge,
Of a man called Gibb and an old log crib
On the top of Hollyburn Ridge;
> And some rumours say that in Horseshoe Bay
> There's the corpse of an old steam boat
> Left, battered and wrecked, where it died of neglect
> Waterlogged, and unable to float.

And there's still some folk who enjoy a joke,
Living up there, who'll swear to the truth
Of a bad-assed gang and the songs they sang
As they searched for the secret of Youth;
> There were nine of these guys and you must realize,
> This was years before Women's Lib . . .
> They were chauvinists all, and just havin' a ball,
> And the ringleader's name was Gibb.
The fifties were nifty, and these guys were thrifty
Yet free, all the same, with a buck,
And they'd bought an old shack, off the well-beaten track
But accessible, still, to a truck,

And there, on weekends, they'd convene with their friends
And they'd raise all kinds of Hell;
They'd be gamblin' and drinkin' and talkin' and thinkin'
And cussin' and swearin' as well!

But one weekend, ol' Buck started pushin' his luck
And got into a fight with a tree;
The tree was much taller and Buck was way smaller
But stubborn? God! Could he be!
    Now, I'm hearing you say to yourselves, "There's no way
    That a grown man can fight with a tree!"
    But if that man can say that that tree's in his way,
    Then a fight has been picked, seems to me!

"I can see that ol' tree's gotta go: It must be
Clear ten feet through the bole, there," thought Buck;
"And the son of a gun blocks the shack from the sun;
An', if ever it falls, well, good luck!
    That tree ought to come down; no point foolin' aroun',
    It's a menace," so Buck up and yelled
    To his good buddies whose eyes were fixed on their booze,
    "C'm'ere, guys! This tree needs to get felled!"

Well, they worked 'til they blew, but not one of them knew
That the heart of that ol' tree was hollow;
It was filled by a rod of dried wood that, by God,
Would hold that old tree up 'til tomorrow!
    The harder they sawed, the more they became awed,
    For that old tree just wouldn't saw through,
    'Cause that plug of dead wood at its centre was good
    As a brace, or a bone splint or two . . .

And then Watson Davis said "Bless us an' save us,
This ain't doin' no good at all.
We've been goin' full power for more than four hours,
An' this sum'bitch ain't ready to fall!"
    And Wayne Heath muttered, "Boys, I'm not one to make noise,

But I've just about had it with this;
Let's give it one more try—one good shove; do or die,
Then let's go and get back on the piss!"

See that tree over there? Check it out, and compare
The weird way that it lines up with this 'un.
Seems to me, if we sight, and then drop it just right,
We can bring 'em both down, Okay? Listen . . ."
  He went on to define how they'd both fall in line
  And lie, side by side, out in the open;
  They'd have firewood galore lying right at the door,
  To be had just by reachin' and gropin'!

Well, the smaller tree fell, and the big one as well,
But, somehow, the direction was wrong,
As Slouch Malcolm stepped back to the door of the shack
He was humming a bit of a song . . .
  He'd been fixing some food, old Slouch cooked pretty good,
  And, still clutching an old, blackened skillet,
  He had stepped to the door to check out the uproar
  And to take out the kettle and fill it . . .

Slouch looked upwards, to see the top of the big tree
Leaning over him, far out of true;
He yelled "Sonofabitch!" and took off, down the stretch
Like a greyhound dog. Well, wouldn't you?
  What he'd seen, he explained later, time and again,
  Was that tree, coming down like a lid!
  That big, ugly old tree would leave only debris
  Where the cabin had been—and it did!

So, they built a new cabin
  And roofed it with cedar
    And forty years rolled by, and more . . .
And they still get together
  For fishin' an' drinkin'
    And poker, as in days of yore . . .

But Buck Gibb's adventures
      Have filled up his dance card
            And now he's arrived at three score ...
Buck is sixty years old and,
      My friends, I've been told
            That he's good for a few dozen more.

149

"To See Ourselves as Others See Us"

(*Used with permission of Anthony Jenkins,* The Globe and Mail)

CHAPTER EIGHT

SASKATCHEWAN

I have not spent a great deal of time in Saskatchewan, but I am delighted to say that every day and every moment I ever spent there was enjoyable in the unforgettable sense, and I truly regret not having made a greater effort to spend more time there.

My wife's people come from Shaunavon, in the southwest region of the province, and she has cousins who live and farm in the wonderful little community of Eastend, 19-odd miles west and south of there. The name comes from its location at the easternmost end of the Cypress Hills, which, for some unexplained reason, escaped the scouring of the glaciers during the most recent ice age and therefore is home to species of flora and fauna that exist nowhere else, giving the region the nickname the Galapagos of Canada.

I can't easily describe what I have come to think of as my South Saskatchewan Experience, because the sensations that swept over me were completely alien to anything I had encountered prior to that time, and I had no experiential yardstick by which to judge them. But they were profound and long-lasting in their effect, so much so that I still find myself thinking from time to time that I ought to drop everything for a while and go back there. The entire region is astonishing. You may be thinking, it's Saskatchewan, for crying out loud, and everyone knows what Saskatchewan's like: flat and featureless and enormous, and prone to bug infestations that would make Alfred Hitchcock shudder.

That's what I thought before I went there. But then I actually went there, and I saw some things the likes of which I had never imagined and others that, while predictable, had about them an undeniable resonance of Twilight Zone unreality. Like the mind-boggling strangeness—strange but not at all unpleasant—of walking through a field of ankle-high stubble and seeing huge cascades of inch-long grasshoppers, thousands upon thousands of them, leaping away from your feet at every step, as if you were splashing heavy-footed through an enormous but shallow puddle of water, kicking the spraying drops far out ahead of you. And the associated thrill—not quite so enjoyable—of looking at the front grill of your fancy, brand-new car and realizing that it is coated with an inches-thick, yellow-and-brown-flecked layer of those same grasshoppers, which you picked up along the 93 miles of highway you travelled since turning south off the Trans-Canada. But you accept that that is Saskatchewan, and if you are anything like me, you throw back your shoulders and inhale all of it, not wanting to miss a single nuance of the atmosphere.

Above and beyond everything else in Saskatchewan, at least in the summers when I used to visit there, there was the Sun, always with a capital "S" in my imaginings, blinding, blazing and mystical in ways that don't appear to register anywhere else. Anyone who has ever been in Saskatchewan during the winter will tell you about the prairie blizzards and how you could get lost and freeze to death between your front door and the outhouse if you didn't rig a rope to guide you there and back. There are all kinds of tales about the wilds of winter, but everyone seems to take Saskatchewan summers for granted, and I find that astonishing because Saskatchewan and its summer sun are unimaginable to people where I came from in Britain. Great fat-bellied carp belching contentedly like Garfield the cat in the warm, dirt-brown irrigation ditches, enormous fields dotted with distant, crawling tractors that, close up, are bigger than the homes of some of their drivers . . . I thought about Saskatchewan, and its summer sun, a lot when I was there.

The Sun King (Le Roi Soleil)

They say mad dogs and Englishmen too frequently go out in him
And rainmakers and shamans daydream constantly of floutin' him
While ski resorts and spas, it seems, will never tire of toutin' him
And surf bums, golfers, and anaemics tend to wax devout in him

Sinuous continental superhighways writhe and melt in him
And vendors of cosmetics all appreciate the gelt in him,
While zebus, gnus, kudus and boks go bouncing o'er the Veldt in him
And many a naive beauty's grown red welts on her svelte pelt in him

Oenophiles and their vintners have a tried and trusted friend in him
Saskatchewan agrologists have met a broiling end in him
Floridans in retirement have all kinds of time to spend in him
And Aussies spend their Christmases, sans snow and ice, defendin' him.

Distilled of immortality (no sun can ever set on him)
He's perfect punctuality (no book would take a bet on him)
If he were on the Stock Exchange I'd buy all I could get on him
And yet, I'll shortly close the door of verse with no regret on him

The Sun, Old Sol, Le Roi Soleil, The Friendly Giant, the Lord of Light
Through pre- and present history, through ages dark and ages bright
The Source of Power, Life-giving Force, the death of darkness, foe of night
The face no man can look upon unaided and retain his sight.

We've honoured and appeased him, supplicated and placated him
Revered him and despised him, worshipped him and even hated him
We've measured him and studied him, we've classified and rated him
And, practicing pollution, virtually emasculated him

But northern Arctic Esquimaux revere him when he comes to call
(Though their equatorial counterparts might doubt the saneness of it all)
And Southern Californians don't ever doubt him—not at all
And neither, for that matter, do the dwellers in Bengal!

154

Nothing, however, could ever match the thrill I felt the first time I visited the junior high school in Eastend, because I had been told that some dinosaur bones were on display there. It must have been in the summer of 1976. I dropped by on a Friday morning at the invitation of one of the local teachers, to look at them. I knew this was dinosaur country, and I knew too that many skeletons had been found here in a place called the White Clay Pit, so I was curious to see what the school had on exhibit.

It was a small school, typical of a small town, but the first thing that struck me upon entering was the width of the hallways and the featureless nature of the walls on either side. They held no paintings or student exhibits of any kind, and I found that very unusual—until I discovered why. There were paintings and exhibits aplenty in other areas of the school, but the main hallways contained large, deep window boxes, six in all, each measuring (as I remember it) approximately six feet wide by six feet high by six feet deep. Inside each of these boxes was a complete triceratops skull, with triple horns and bony carapaces, enormous, awe-inspiring things whose presence here in a small-town school's hallway was far more astounding and impressive than it could ever have been in a great museum. They were gigantic, alien and bizarre, and chilling in their monstrous hugeness, with eye sockets that could engulf a large man's fist, and great long horns that were six to eight inches in diameter where they joined the skull. And they were here, enshrined without fanfare in this small-town school.

That same year I went driving into the trackless prairie in my host's old pickup truck one brilliant summer afternoon and found a teepee ring on a raised spur of hillside. It had been there for a long time, for among the circle of stones used to anchor the coverings, I found a knapped-flint spearhead, several flint arrowheads and many crude stone hand tools—split pebbles with their scraping edges encrusted with a long-dried residue of buffalo fat. I stood in the centre of the ring, in what was once the fireplace, wondering how long it had been since anyone else had stood there, and I looked out across the hugeness of that rolling landscape and tried to visualize what it would have been like to live there alone, never seeing a stranger for months or years on end.

Later that same day, four or five miles from the teepee ring, I steered cautiously around the flank of a treacherous, rock-strewn slope and found an enormous pile of cattle bones in a small, hidden valley; uncountable bones, piled in great white heaps. My first thought was that I had found a buffalo jump, but then I realized that there was no high cliff from which the animals could have been driven to their death. The valley was a shallow, rock-sided bowl, pressed into the surrounding hillside as though the hill had once been made of dough, and it had only one entrance, the one I had used. And about that time I realized, too, that the desiccated horns I could see were bovine, not bison, horns. One of the local old-timers nodded when I mentioned it that night, over a beer in the local bar, and said he knew the place. An enormous herd of cattle, more than 200 head, had been

155

blown into that dead end—he called it a canyon—ahead of a blizzard in 1906, he said. Unable to go any farther once they were in there, they had simply bunched up and died, covered by the snow, and had not been found until the following spring, when they thawed and began to rot. Thereafter, my imagination kick-started by his comment, I spent hours trying to visualize what that scene must have smelled and looked like in the spring of 1907. I finally decided that the impossibility of imagining it was an integral part of the overwhelming impact of this place called Saskatchewan.

Saskatchewan

For years, 'til now, the story ran
That nothing in Saskatchewan
Endeared the place to beast or man;
That nothing was, but space.
There, emptinesses froze the mind;
The winter's blizzards blew in kind;
The dust storms rendered watchers blind
And sane men shunned the place.

Only a few, a loyal few
Endured and stayed to learn and grew
To love Saskatchewan and knew
The beauties of her face;
For, when she smiles, her countenance
Is open, loving, and her glance
Will melt your heart and brace your stance
With pride, and strength, and grace.

Then you forget what's gone before,
The caterpillars, bugs galore,
The grasshoppers who swarm and soar
To hide the sun's white face.
Forgotten are her cruel ways,

The crushing snows, the frost's harsh glaze,
The brushfires, hailstorms, dust bowl days,
For glory fills this place.

South, there, among the Cypress hills,
Perspectives change, enchantment thrills,
And deer drink where the river spills
And stately herons pace.
Saskatchewan; a giant name;
A giant land man can not tame
No matter how he rigs his game
Or tries to run his race.

Man knows that he is blessed to be
In that fair land at all; that he
Should be content to be there, free
And living in God's Grace.

Jack Whyte as Robbie Burns, with Catherine MacKinnon and Andy Stewart, on the set of the CBC variety show *The Maple and the Thistle* (1975)

CHAPTER NINE

BRITISH COLUMBIA

My first visit to British Columbia, to Vancouver, left me unimpressed. I remember it well. It was a wet and windy day in February 1975, and the city was not at its most beauteous. A cold wind was coming off the water, the streets seemed to be ankle deep in sodden leaves from the previous autumn, and kitty-corner from the CBC building at the main post office, which was closed down by a strike, a moving chain of shivering, miserable, placard-carrying members added its own brand of *je ne sais quoi* to what was generally a pretty drab and depressing panorama.

I was in the city because I had been summoned to meet with Jack McAndrew, who was then head of CBC Television Variety. I had flown in from Calgary that morning at an ungodly hour, on the first flight available, for a 10:00 A.M. appointment. It had been pouring rain when I landed, and it was still dark as I made my way by taxi from the airport to the CBC building, arriving there before eight o'clock. I was ravenously hungry and looking forward to a nourishing breakfast, but I was too early: the cafeteria had not yet opened. It's hard to imagine, but there were no Starbucks outlets in those days;

the coffee-shop phenomenon lay years in the future.

As a stranger in the city, then, my options were to remain where I was and wait for the cafeteria to open at eight, or go trudging off through the rain in hope of stumbling across a place where I might be able to find something to eat. It was a no-brainer. I stayed where I was, shuddering with self-pity under a glass canopy in the courtyard of austere concrete and glass that was the CBC building, and eventually the cafeteria did open and I was permitted to scuttle inside. By that time, I had watched the sky gradually lighten as the sun rose somewhere behind the solid layer of grey overhead, and I had taken close and critical note of the new day's stirrings and of the unfriendly aloofness of the swarming people who would, I felt, have trodden me underfoot if I had been in their way. And so, to pass the time, I sat in the cafeteria that morning and wrote "Early Bird."

Early Bird

Bitter coffee on a winter morning;
Colourless Vancouver.
Nothing is shining,
Or even glistening.
The red-tiled courtyard of the CBC
Is wet in places,
Puddled in others;
Dull puddles of stale water.
The fountain doesn't.
Discarded and drowned,
The corpses of last summer's leaves
Are huddled everywhere.
Suddenly it is eight thirty
And the courtyard is awash
With a proliferation of beards
And groovy briefcases
Without handles

As the working brains of CBC
Salute the circle-C in passing
And scurry into the glass-and-concrete
Warren
Of Headquarters.
Regional Headquarters,
British Columbia.
One can see, after all,
Why Columbia had to be British . . .
The sky is a wash
Of leaden grey
Spread over fog-steel.
A gull glides gracefully
And staggers in flight
Apparently wracked
With coughing.
At a neighbouring table
A distinguished-looking,
Pin-stripe-suited man
Is discoursing, low voiced and intense,
On Niggers!
Even the women in the courtyard
Seem to have beards.
Everything's frightfully Arty!
Someone switched on the wind.
In the square outside
The flags begin to flap.
The B.C. Sun, the Maple Leaf
And the million-dollar "C".
Brown bag lunches are clutched
In most of the entering hands.
So much for fancy cafeteriae!
Enter one small pipe-smoking,
Blue-coated, yellow-gloved
Horn-rimmed, short-haired,
Richly-shoed Executive!
The pipe severely gripped

Between the teeth
Thrusts forward like a bowsprit
And from the lenses of the horn-rimmed eyes
Sparks leap to meet
This day's exigencies.
Woe to the timid,
Weak-willed underling
Who stumbles in this paragon's
Forceful path!

His very bearing seems to indicate
That men must use iambics in his ken
And couch those iambs in pentameters
Here comes a maiden lady, fifty-ish,
Swathed in fur hat, cloth coat
And low-heeled shoes,
Her mouth a down-turned
Disapproving line
Denoting misery to all
Who come within
Her dowdy, disenchanted grasp.
Perhaps she smiled once,
In the long ago,
But nothing would permit
Her frozen glare
To break into a softening warmth today.
My coffee's cold;
The weather's drab,
But why am I so down?
I should be glad.
I have been called
To join the chosen few!
My talents are required!
And here I sit
And watch and wait
And wait . . .

Despite the day's depressing start, my meeting was a great success, launching me along another enjoyable and successful byway in my writing career. Jack McAndrew had seen me perform my Robbie Burns show at the National Arts Centre in Ottawa and had been impressed enough to think of me a few months later when something unusual came up. CBC Television had contracted to produce a 90-minute variety show starring Andy Stewart, who would fly in from Scotland for the 10 days of production involved. Catherine McKinnon, then "Canada's Singing Sweetheart," would be Andy's foil, and a young Scots tenor from Victoria, BC, Bill Hosie, would provide local west coast support. The trouble was, they didn't have a vehicle to build the show around, and since it needed to be Scottish—to some extent at least—Jack thought of me and of Robbie Burns. He knew I had written *Rantin', Rovin' Robin*, but now he was wondering whether I could write a TV variety show starring the aforementioned luminaries and featuring myself somehow as the ghost of Burns in a way that would pull the entire show together.

Well, we called the show *The Maple and the Thistle*, and it was a celebration of the Scottish influence in and on Canada. It originally had a bare-bones budget, so there was to be nothing elaborate about it, but when the production people saw the script I had come up with, they went overboard on the set. They built a Highlands hillside, complete with running stream and a thatched cottage, on one side of the studio, and the full drawing room of a Scottish baronial mansion on the other, with a magnificent fireplace on one wall and tall windows opposite it that opened out onto the hillside. The entire rear length of the studio became a street of Scottish tenements. It was a phenomenally successful show, and because of it I wrote a number of equally successful "SuperSpecials," as they were known, over the next couple of years. My favourite was a show called *Let Us*

163

Remember, which starred Will Millar and the Irish Rovers and featured a visit by Dame Vera Lynn to the Star and Garter Veterans' Hospital in Vancouver. For this show, the director, Ken Gibson, asked me to come up with a different approach to the Remembrance Day message, something to bring out the solemnity and the reality underlying it. The result was quite spectacular.

My favourite uncle, also a Jack Whyte, was living in the Chateau Vimy at this time, right below Vimy Ridge, and was the senior man—I suppose he would have been a civil servant, although I've never thought about that before—in charge of the entire Somme Division of the Commonwealth War Graves Commission (formerly called the Imperial War Graves Commission). I had visited Uncle Jack in France many times during my student days in the early '60s and had seen the Somme battlefields in great detail—far greater detail than most people are ever allowed to see. The impressions they had left had proved indelible, so when it came time to produce "something different" for this particular show, I remembered the power of what I had experienced at Somme and conceived the idea of using some of the poems written by the First World War poets who first saw modern warfare as the horrific and terrifying reality it was and moved rapidly away from the jingoistic "Up, Boys, And At 'Em" style of touting warfare as a wonderful thing to which all young men should aspire. We considered war poet Wilfred Owen's harrowing piece "Gas Attack," the strongest anti-war statement written during the First World War, and decided to dramatize it using professional actors.

I contacted my uncle in his official capacity and told him what I was thinking of doing. The upshot is that a film team was dispatched from Vancouver to Vimy Ridge, and from the footage it brought back, CBC set designers were able to construct an absolutely authentic replica of a Canadian First World War trench in Vimy, complete with dugouts. There, in silent slow motion, to the accompaniment of a powerful, voice-over reading of Owen's poem and against a murky, swirling background of yellowish green smoke, we filmed the soldiers' panicky scramble to find gas masks as canisters of deadly mustard gas began to land among them. It was a powerful show, and it was chosen that year as Canada's entry to the Golden Rose Festival of Television in Montreux, Switzerland.

It was the final scene I found most moving and memorable: a Canadian soldier stands motionless, head lowered, in a trench. He is wearing a rain slicker, buttoned up to the neck, and the hammering of the rain is the only sound as the water pours in a steady stream from the rim of his steel helmet, down his poncho and into the ankle-deep pool of muddy water in which he is standing. He holds his rifle muzzle down, against his chest, to protect it from rain and mud, and as the notes of the last post finally begin to sound above the downpour, he blinks once, and his thick, beautiful blond eyelashes stand in stark contrast to the relentless ugliness and lifelessness of the landscape in which he is imprisoned.

Ironically, it was during the filming of that show with the Irish Rovers that I first saw Vancouver in the sunshine and realized what an astoundingly beautiful place it is. I took Beverley out to visit Will Millar's lovely home on the cliffs of West Vancouver one stunning afternoon, and Will took us to Lighthouse Park, a little farther down the coast, and showed us the tree that inspired my poem "Lighthouse Park."

Lighthouse Park

We walked, three people, through a silent place
With dead leaves underfoot, and all around
Was stillness, unrelieved and absolute

And I was hard put to believe I'd found
Such solitude, such splendour and such grace.

There were the three of us; my Love, myself,
And a soft-spoken, mystic Leprechaun
Who murmured of Love's Labours and the fruit
That vanishes in tasting and is gone,
Leaving an empty, dusty, larder shelf.

This man, this magic spirit whom the world
Sees as an elfin figure of delight,
Spoke of, and took us with him to behold,
A thing that calms him, sets his mind aright
When into Hell by life his soul seems hurled.

There, by the path's side, stands a mighty tree
That sweeps the eye to where the neck might break:
A Douglas Fir, five and more centuries old,
Admonishing that for Man's soul's sweet sake
He should remember Earth holds more than he.

Before Columbus brought the pale-skinned race
To walk with alien feet this magic land,
Before the European nations shook
Their conquering fists or stretched a grasping hand,
This mighty tree was standing in this place.

We gazed at those five hundred living years
With an hypnotic surge of disbelief
And stunned, we turned ourselves around and took
Our little problems homewards with relief,
Too glad of life to waste our time with tears.

British Columbia has always had a way of splashing me with inspiration in the strangest places and at the oddest times. In 1994, soon after completing a CD called *80 Years of Glory with the Pipes and Drums of the Calgary Highlanders*, I was asked to write a piece that I eventually came to believe had defeated my abilities. The CD was commemorative, featuring the pipes and drums of the regiment with me, as the regimental bard, reciting the poems I had written for the Highlanders. It had been prepared in honour of the 80th anniversary of the raising of the regiment and the presentation and "trooping" of the new regimental colours in 1990 by Her Majesty Queen Elizabeth. I had been flown back to Calgary to serve as the emcee/commentator for the trooping the colour ceremony.

On that occasion, at a gathering afterwards in the regimental officers' mess, then-pipe major Bob Henderson buttonholed me and bent my ear about writing lyrics for what was then one of the best-known and most recognizable bagpipe tunes in the world, a piece called "Highland Cathedral." The melody had been written by a German bagpiper some time earlier, but no one had ever written lyrics for the tune. The pipe major wanted me to write lyrics and then record them with the band on a future CD. And at the time, flushed beyond caution with the consumption of a second glass of sherry, I agreed to do it.

Looking back on it, that was probably the single most frustrating project I ever undertook, because I could not make it work, although not for lack of trying. One of the first things I discovered, going into the earliest stages of my research, was that there *are* no great Highland cathedrals, certainly nothing along the lines of the great English cathedrals of Ely and York, or Lincoln and Canterbury. I had visions of ruined grandeur and tapering, windowless arches casting shadows and attracting sunbeams, like the scenes of Melrose Abbey and other medieval ruins that one sees, but there was nothing there, no galvanizing spark, to get my creative juices flowing. For months I worked on that little project, growing more and more annoyed and frustrated that I couldn't find anything to sink my creative teeth into. I must have started 50 different versions, and all of them, one after the other, went into the circular file drawer until eventually I gave up and abandoned the idea.

But a couple of months after that, Beverley and I took a two-week vacation at a little resort called Two Coves, on Vancouver Island just south of Nanaimo. Our neighbours had spent a couple of weeks there and recommended the place to us, and we decided on the spur of the moment to try it. We got lucky, calling in just after Two Coves had received a cancellation. It was a splendid place, and we had a wonderful time there, eating superb fresh Yellow Point corn drenched in butter every night because it was in season and cost 25 cents an ear. One beautiful evening we took a boat and went out fishing, and as often happens when you're fishing and having fun, time got away on us so that all of a sudden it was getting late and we had to get back to shore. I turned the boat around and headed in, sailing west into one of the most gorgeous sunsets I had ever seen, and there, in massed, magnificent colour, was my Highland cathedral—the mountains of Vancouver Island.

Highland Cathedral

Look to the mountains when you turn to pray;
Think how they reach to Heaven every day,
Lifting their snowy heads and shoulders broad;
Offering all they are to the eyes of God.

Misty and mystic in the morning light;
Painted with colour in the noonday bright;
Golden and purple in the evening air;
All day and every day mountains stand in prayer.

Lift your eyes and see where they rise
Higher and higher, steeple and spire;
Buttress, gable and soaring tower,
Dwarfing Man's earthly power!

These are Cathedrals that no man could build;
Awesome and glorious and wonder-filled;
Each is a masterpiece, each one unique,
Living a prayer, though lacking a voice to speak.

So look to the mountains when you turn to pray;
See how they strive for Heaven every day,
Lifting their snowy heads and shoulders broad,
Offering all they are to the eyes of God.

I can't move on from here without harking back one more time
to Calgary and the trooping the colour ceremony in 1990, because in
the course of it I saw one of the most brilliant and effective pieces of
public relations and goodwill-building that I have ever witnessed. I was
up in the broadcast booth on the top of the grandstand, where I had a
superb view of the entire stadium, and I had a Queen's equerry/aide-
de-camp up there with me to keep an eye on matters of protocol and to
prompt me on what I might, might not, must and must not say.

I had a complete script detailing who the VIP guests were and
why they were here, and I would be tipped off by radio as each of
them drove into the stadium in a limousine to make a tour of the
arena to the music of whatever military band was playing at the time. I
would then tell the people in the bleachers who each newcomer was.
It worked smoothly and the audience loved it, applauding warmly and
enthusiastically as each guest disembarked from his or her limo.

And then I got the word, "General de Chastelain's here. He's coming in now." De Chastelain, who had always been a soldier's soldier, was at that time chief of the defence staff, the highest-ranking soldier in Canada's military. I had known he was coming in because the regimental pipes and drums had just changed formation and were preparing to escort him to his place of honour once he climbed out of his car. As the limo made its circuit, I read the commentary on the general, delineating his career and achievements and concluding by pointing out a piece of trivia that not one person in a thousand of the people there could have known: the general had begun his military career as a cadet piper in the Calgary Highlanders regiment.

That brought a collective "Ooh!" of wonder that was audible even in the booth where I was, but the best was yet to come, and it was something that even I had not expected. I had met the general a couple of times at regimental functions, and I knew that he was a delightful man, amazingly and refreshingly lacking in stuffiness. But on this occasion, he made me smile and shake my head with admiration, for he climbed out of the back of the limo in full uniform, not as chief of defence staff for Canada, but as a corporal piper in the Calgary Highlanders. He saluted the rostrum and the assembled guests, inflated his pipes and joined the band, marching with the regimental pipes and drums for the first time since he was a boy. The hair stood up on the nape of my neck. I had been in the advertising and public-relations arena for years, but I had never seen anything to equal that. And I never have since.

But now back to BC, and to Vancouver in particular. I did change my mind about it being a dreadful place, although only gradually, after visiting a few more times and discovering that it was not always raining or about to rain, that the sun had been known to break through the clouds on the odd occasion. But my real epiphany occurred in 1985, when I had occasion to go there on business in early March, when

Alberta is still firmly locked in the clutches of winter. I stepped off the plane in Vancouver and was stunned to discover that the weather was mild and warm, the sunshine was breathtaking, and every tree in the Lower Mainland seemed to be covered with blossoms of pink, yellow or white. There were magnolia trees blooming everywhere I looked, and the ground was ablaze with daffodils, tulips, jonquils and an amazing array of azalea shrubs of every colour. I was stupefied, completely unable to assimilate what I was seeing or to rationalize why I would live in an interior, continental climate when I could be living here. My epiphany, I understand, was not unique. I was far from being the first person to undergo that sea change, and as long as there is sunshine there will never be a last one, either. The damage was done, and I went home and told Beverley that I was moving to the coast and she was welcome to come with me.

As it turned out, we did not move immediately, but I commuted for a year, working on contract as communications director for a company called Johnston Terminals. I spent the entire summer of 1986 living in a hotel on Granville Island, which was still in the process of being reclaimed from the grime and grunge of 100 years of industrial abuse and transformed into a lively, bustling centre of arts and entertainment.

Granville Island Impressionism

kaleidoscope, cacophony, confusion,
seething, heaving, bustling busyness;
a potpourri anthology of medleys en pastiche:
key changes, segues, tinny modulations
shape-shifting styles and sights and sounds and smells;
rusting cranes, looming bridges, railroad tracks
and heavy iron bollards in the streets;
restaurants, cafés, bistros, bars, boutiques;
offices, studios, hostelries;

playhouses, plazas and potteries;
cobblestones; small, neat lawns and tree-lined parks;
waterways clear, uncluttered, clean and well maintained
and heavy trucks and barges hauling concrete;
houseboats, moored yachts and buskers,
popcorn and creosote scents on hot afternoons;
performances in squares and clowns on piers and jugglers among market stalls,
pointing the smells of food and fresh baked bread;
and people everywhere, to and fro

172

between the cars in covered parking lots
that once were factories,
grim, Victorian windows stark
among the weltering colours all around;
yesterday, today and tomorrow in one gulp . . .

On a street corner in West Vancouver there is a fountain that I believe to be the most beautiful of its kind anywhere. It is made from one enormous block of stone, and it reminds me of a dear and long-dead friend called Joyce Elliott, whose full name was Joyce Alison Denman Elliott, JADE for short. Joyce was a poet and a great reader, and she signed her poetry as JADE. The fountain is an enormous lump of solid jade, and I would never dream of going to Vancouver nowadays without going to the North Shore just to look at it again and to lay my palm on the unbelievably smooth, polished channel in the rock and let the soothing water flow over it.

In memory of my friend JADE—Joyce A. D. Elliott

On a corner in West Vancouver,
Just off the edge of a busy, bustling street,
There is a fountain with a beauty quite unique . . .
A monolith; one stone, pristine,
Brought from the mountains and installed in town,
Pierced with a single channel to hold copper pipes.

Rugged, and shapeless in the way of rocks,
Pale, whitish, grey-grained green, and weathered by the years,
It sits within a frame of man-made walls,
And flows, year-round, producing beauty,
Pleasuring all who pass, or stop to look,
Or listen to its welling, liquid sounds.

Unremarkable at first glance, apparently unimpressive
Lacking distinction save for its formlessness,
Plain, commonplace and earthy like a piece of shale,
This enigmatic boulder goes unmarked,
Except by those whose eyes look down, beyond its surface
Into its glowing soul . . .
It is a giant gemstone, subtly rich, with a dense, deep, lambent, burnished inner glow.

Out of its surface, laying bare its depths,
Piercing its plainness to expose its soul,
Someone has carved a wedge
And polished the hidden heart there, bringing out
Beauty beyond belief : lacework, and tight-scrolled textures, thick and dense,
      lacquered and light and lovely;
Patinaed, green-glazed vistas of solid, smooth, petrified seascapes in the living
      stone;
Multi-dimensioned soundness, deep-hued calm, offering coolness on the warmest
      day;
Wisdom and ageless beauty and timeless charm, soaring above the norm of
      common clay.

Soothing each passing soul like a healing balm, spreading a quiet joy in its lustrous way,
Standing in silence, as a living prayer, it offers solace in reality—
Reminding me that I knew, and was blessed to know,
Another Jade.

Soon after Beverley and I moved to Vancouver, we began looking
for a house to buy, and since we were not at all sure where we wanted
to live, we searched throughout the Lower Mainland, including New

Westminster, which at the start of 1986 was just beginning to flex its muscles and adjust to the new demands for expansion that were starting to transform the entire Lower Mainland. We eventually settled on Vancouver's North Shore, but New Westminster made an indelible impression upon me, partly because of my friend Bill McKinney and his beloved Royal Westminster Regiment, but also because of its impressive early history, when it almost became the capital city of British Columbia.

174

I had a friend who lived there and was totally in love with the city— Mike Paul, another Scot and a talented musician who ran a Scottish country dance band. Mike had written a dance tune, a waltz, in honour of his city, but being neither writer nor poet, he had never made any attempt to set lyrics to it. When he and I got to know each other, however, introduced by our mutual friend Rob Stuart, he asked me if I would consider writing words for his tune "The New Westminster Waltz." I said I would, and as I settled down to mull, I found that the words were already there, in my mind, assembled years earlier and awaiting only the summons to trot forth. I enjoyed writing the lyrics, and I enjoyed singing them, although I have not done so in years. In revisiting the song recently, with this book in mind, I realized it would make a fitting conclusion to my reminiscences on the last four decades, because it deals with the specifics of living in western Canada, and its content spans far more time than it takes to sing the song. More than anything else, however, I think this little song reflects the pride, the affection and the gratitude with which I acknowledge and embrace my life as a 40-year Canadian.

New Westminster Waltz

Come, walk by my side, friend, and listen to me
And I'll sing you a song of my home in B.C.
That's British Columbia in Canada's West
Where God's in His heaven and man's at his best:

There, south of Vancouver, the Fraser rolls wide
And mingles its silt with the ocean's salt tide
And Steveston fishermen ply up and down
The channel that fronts New Westminster town.

Where British Columbia slopes to the sea
The lights of New Westminster beckon to me
And, deep in my bosom, wherever I roam
I carry my proud Canadian home.

Go, travel the world, lad, my grandfather said,
Go, gaze upon beauty and fill up your head
With all of the glories man's made on this earth,
But never forget the place of your birth;

Go, travel the oceans, explore distant lands;
Experience the world, hold its wealth in your hands;
Grow rich upon all that your mind can contain
And then turn around and head home again

Where British Columbia slopes to the sea
New Westminster town will be waiting for ye;
And, deep in your breast, lad, wherever you roam,
You'll remember your proud Canadian home . . .

I've wandered through Paris and Old Montreal
I've chewed the Big Apple and swallowed it all;
I loved Acapulco, I hated Algiers
And old Copenhagen moved me to tears

I've flown down to Rio, I just couldn't wait;
I've crossed 'Frisco Bay by the great Golden Gate;
I've stared at Miami and London and Rome
And smiled with the thought, There's no place like Home!

Where British Columbia slopes to the sea
The lights of New Westminster beckon to me
And, deep in my bosom, wherever I roam
I carry my proud Canadian home . . .

176

ACKNOWLEDGEMENTS

It would take more space than I have in this book to acknowledge properly all the people I have thought of with pleasure, affection and nostalgia as I wrote this little memoir, which is why I decided instead to tip my hat to all of them in the dedication.

There are, however, several people not mentioned in this book whom I simply must acknowledge for their contributions to my life and my experience. Many of them, unfortunately, are dead now, people like Dr. Grant MacEwan of Calgary, the greatest Canadian I have had the privilege of knowing, who gave me one of the best pieces of advice I ever got after I told him back in 1994 that I was considering returning to university for postgraduate studies. "Forget that," he snapped, raising an eyebrow in protest. "You've written four wonderful novels. Keep writing more, and sooner or later, somebody will *give* you a Ph.D."

Fred Mannix of Calgary was honorary colonel of the Calgary Highlanders when I stepped aboard as regimental bard, and I have derived great pleasure from our association ever since then, travelling frequently to his winter quarters in southern California on or around the 25th of January in order to regale his Robbie Burns Night guests with the songs, poetry and exploits of the Ploughman Bard. Were it not for Fred and his influence, I would never have written my songs and poems for the Calgary Highlanders.

The late Robert Wilson, chairman of the ill-fated Northland Bank when I approached it in the late 1980s, decided that my work was far better qualified for promotion and support than the vast majority of *pro bono* concerns that he and the bank were asked to finance every week, so he steered me through the process of seeking and gaining a loan—struggling, unpublished authors are by definition insolvent, and *personae non gratae* in banking circles. That loan enabled me to dedicate a whole year to completing my first novel. The book was bigger than anticipated, however, and it grew into three novels—eventually, into a nine-book cycle. Those books might never have been written without Robert's intercession and his belief in my abilities.

Then there's my pal Bill McKay, formerly of Calgary and now a resident of Vancouver. It was Billy who imported me to Vancouver to write the corporate history of Johnston Terminals; that project provided me with tons of research material for a someday novel on the industrial development of the Canadian west coast and the rise of the union movement in the early 20th century. And it was there, in Vancouver, that I completed the transition from entertainer and musician to full-time author. Bill and I have been up and down a few roads together and shared a lot of laughs and pleasure since we first met in the early 1970s.

And I would be remiss not to mention Ray Addington, former chairman of Kelly-Douglas Corporation, whom I met originally through Bill McKay. Ray brought me one of my most treasured possessions from Britain, even before I had sold my first books to a publisher. In the town of Colchester, which was the first Roman town in Britain and was featured prominently in my first novel, he put together a collection of five Roman sesterces—small copper coins equivalent to modern pennies—dating from the same period in which Publius Varrus, the narrator of my first two books, lived. A wonderful, thoughtful gift that I appreciate still.

There are many others, living and dead, who deserve acknowledgement, and I know that after this book is in print, I will be thinking with chagrin of people I have missed and ought to have mentioned, so if any of you reading this right now are thinking, "What about me?" I'm sorry.

BOOKS BY JACK WHYTE

A Dream of Eagles series (*The Camolud Chronicles* in the US)
The Skystone (1992)
The Singing Sword (1993)
The Eagles' Brood (1994)
The Saxon Shore (1995)
The Sorcerer Vol. I: The Fort at River's Bend (1997)
The Sorcerer Vol. II: Metamorphosis (1997)
Uther (2000)
Clothar the Frank (*The Lance Thrower* outside Canada) (2003)
The Eagle (2005)

Knights Templar Trilogy
Knights of the Black and White (2006)
Standard of Honor (2007)
Order in Chaos (2008)